CLASSIC
TRAMPING
IN NEW ZEALAND

Tramper descending to Blue Lake from Moss Pass (SB).

CLASSIC
TRAMPING
IN NEW ZEALAND

SHAUN BARNETT & ROB BROWN

CRAIG
POTTON
PUBLISHING

Text and photographs (except where otherwise credited):
Shaun Barnett and Rob Brown.
Project coordinator: Robbie Burton.
Editing: James Brown and David Chowdhury.
Layout and maps: Tina Delceg.
Filmwork: Astra Print Ltd.
Printing: Everbest Printing Co., Hong Kong.

Published by Craig Potton Publishing, Box 555, Nelson, New Zealand.
©1999 Shaun Barnett and Rob Brown.
©credited photographers.

ISBN 0 908802 51 X (softcover)
ISBN 0 908802 50 1 (hardback)

Land Information New Zealand Map Licence 21363/002

CONTENTS

ACKNOWLEDGEMENTS

This book could not have been published without the assistance and input of many people who share a passion for backcountry tramping. The authors would firstly like to thank Dave Chowdhury whose editorial guidance helped shape the prose of two photographers setting out on the intimidating task of producing a text. The finishing editorial touches were ably done by James Brown. Robbie Burton championed the project from the start and, with the help of the team at Craig Potton Publishing, in particular Tina Delceg, guided the project through to publication.

The final visual look of the book has been greatly enhanced by Nick Groves, Andris Apse, Craig Potton, Robin Smith, Darryn Pegram, Elise Bryant, Scott Freeman and Steve Baker who kindly allowed us to publish some of their photographs.

There are a number of quotes used in the text and appreciation for permission to use these is extended to Brian Turner, Bob Brown and Dorothy Pascoe (for permission to use the John Pascoe quotes). There are a number of definitions in the Tramping Terminology at the back of the book which Geoff Spearpoint allowed us to borrow from his book *Waking to the Hills*.

Many people accompanied the authors on a number of the journeys over the last five years (or was it the authors tagging along?). Many thanks go to the following people for often carrying more than their fair share of party gear and enabling the authors to load their packs up with extra camera equipment: Darryn Pegram, Steve Baker, Rachael Bryce, Mark Schwarz, Louise Thornley, Sharyn Stilwell, John Abbott, Alec Toleafoa, Gin Bush, Mark and Kevin Feeney, Tim Kerr, Clare O'Neill, Grant Singleton, Sally Brown and Daryl Ball – all wonderful companions in the hills. Extra appreciation goes to the people who helped out with photography and were patient in even the foulest weather. All the photos taken of Tim will one day be assembled into an amusing slide show, though only one appears in the book.

Macpac Wilderness Equipment lent early support to this project and over the past few years have provided valuable assistance with equipment. There were many days when tramping was made more comfortable by having equipment designed to meet the demands of the New Zealand environment.

Thanks also to Blair Jacobs (aka Captain Freedom) for bringing us supper (freshly scaled and filleted) at Supper Cove, and Helen and Al at DOC Makarora for a much welcomed cup of tea after another tiring trip in the hills. Sean Husheer (DOC Turangi) and Eddie Te Kahika (DOC Puketitiri) also provided useful information for the Kaweka-Kaimanawa chapter.

Shaun would like to thank his parents Karen and Grant Barnett who, as always, provided encouragement to follow his passion and practical assistance with transport; and especially to Tania for her support and for putting up with his frequent, long absences in the hills.

And finally a special thanks from Rob to Elise who looked after Ben and Shimba while he was away and who in the holidays, when she thought the plan was to go tramping, didn't expect to also be taken on a journey to the planet patience.

The excerpt from *Poem in the Matukituki Valley* by James K. Baxter is reproduced by permission of Oxford University Press Australia and New Zealand and Mrs J. Baxter from *Collected Poems James K. Baxter,* Oxford University Press 1980 © The Estate of James K. Baxter.

ABOUT THIS BOOK

There are many tramping trips in New Zealand that could justifiably be called classic and narrowing them down to twelve seemed, at times, to be inviting the scorn of our fellow trampers. We quickly decided the best approach would be to select twelve journeys which give a good feel for the range of experiences available in the New Zealand backcountry. A diversity of landscapes was selected from coastal (Hollyford), volcanic (Pouakai), and alpine (Copland) to supplement the more traditional 'bush and tops' trips like the Kaweka-Kaimanawa and Nelson Lakes tramps.

The twelve selected tramps also reflect a range of difficulty levels, which trampers may choose to progress through. Tramps like the Hollyford, the Tararua Peaks, and the Pouakai Ranges all offer an excellent network of huts, tracks and bridges which safely give novice trampers the opportunities to gain skills and experience. The hardest level of tramping represented in this book are those tramps which require either the skills to safely negotiate glaciated alpine passes (the Copland Track) or those tramps that follow sparsely marked routes on the edge of wilderness areas with few track and hut facilities (the Five Passes).

Perhaps the most obvious omission in the final selection was a Stewart Island tramp, and the reasons for this are twofold. Firstly, *Classic Tramping* has always been intended to complement Craig Potton's *Classic Walks,* and while there are many trips on Stewart Island, we felt he beautifully covered the main journey there: the gloriously muddy North-west Circuit. Secondly, the rest of Stewart Island still remains steeped in a certain mystery and there was a strong argument for leaving it just so.

Through both the writing and photography a conscious effort has been made to convey not only the essence of the twelve tramps but also to celebrate the whole culture of tramping in New Zealand. We wanted to continue the publishing tradition begun with books like John Pascoe's *Land Uplifted High* (1952) and more lately continued by Geoff Spearpoint's *Waking to the Hills* (1985) and Mark Pickering's *The Hills* (1988). To those lucky enough to own copies, these titles have pride of place on the bookshelf and continue to inspire many trampers to plan their own adventures. It is our sincere hope that *Classic Tramping* is a book which not only serves as a memento for those who have their own experiences on the twelve tramps, but also continues a tradition of celebrating this spirit of the hills.

Finally, the feel of these tracks is often heavily dependent on the number (or lack) of people flocking to them in the short summer season. In selecting twelve classic tramps we were aware we would be encouraging more people to visit, which could degrade some of their remote or wild feel. It is perhaps a naive wish, but we hope this book doesn't encourage people to treat these tramps merely as a tick list, and instead encourages them to plan their own variations to the standard routes. Further, we have tried to communicate the beauty of these tracks in the winter, autumn and spring seasons. Finally, there are thousands of kilometres of track out there, 365 days in most years, more than a thousand basic bridges, over eight hundred huts and numerous rock shelters. With these options tramping in New Zealand is limited only by your imagination, so we urge you to define your own classic tramp.

INTRODUCTION

Our friends across the Tasman call it bushwalking. Visitors from the Northern Hemisphere refer to it as trekking or hiking. In New Zealand, heading off into the wilds with packs loaded for several days has long been referred to as tramping, a term which might seem mildly eccentric – until you visit the landscape. It is the rugged nature of the land which has shaped New Zealand's tramping culture and which also dictates the slow plodding movement sometimes necessary to move steadily through the backcountry on foot. Stumbling over tree roots, easing along a craggy ridge, or scrambling up a streambed of boulders is not everyone's idea of enjoyable travel, but such is the nature of New Zealand tracks that tramping is a more apt description for it than others.

Shaun and I had been heading off into the hills for a long time before we embarked on this project, often without thinking too much about why we did it. Then, as we were struggling, with diminishing enthusiasm, through the thick forest of the Otoko Valley in the Hooker/Landsborough Wilderness Area (a tramp not in this book), we began to wonder what possible purpose the challenge of tramping could serve – particularly in a place without tracks or huts, labouring under 30 kilogram packs in heavy rain, and with the river boulders getting larger and more and more difficult to get around.

It's during these sorts of experiences that you ask the questions most obvious to non-trampers: Why go tramping? Why leave modern comforts for an experience which is sometimes much less than comfortable? The answers are as diverse as they are changeable. What draws me back to the hills involves many different thoughts and emotions; when I'm in the hills, I find these changing in intensity day by day.

One of the more elemental reasons for going tramping is for the sheer joy of exercise in a natural setting. Our jobs keep many of us deskbound, so it is no coincidence that at weekends or during holidays the majority of trampers are from the city. Most of us live with varying degrees of dislocation from the land; tramping then has become a pastime which taps deep desires to renew our contact with nature.

Secondly, and in a way related, trampers seek an experience that is the converse of their urban lives, one where they get by with less, limited by what can be carried in a pack. A week in the hills is one of minimalism where you go without electricity or television, live on a simple diet, and even reduce your fossil fuel consumption to virtually zero (cooking fuel excepted!). It is, as Tasmanian environmentalist Bob Brown has expressed, an experience "where we reach to the mossy edge of a stream for refreshment rather than across a counter".

Once in the hills a third motivation can be felt – the desire to see new landscapes. I have rarely been tramping with anyone who did not enjoy the view from a high point or who, despite being tired and out of breath, did not keep climbing to see the view down the other side. Some say maps and guides have destroyed our abil-

Kiwi Saddle Hut, Kahurangi National Park (RB).

Crossing McCullough Pass, Hooker/Landsborough Wilderness Area (RB).

ity to explore, but for many this does not hold true. Looking at maps and photographs for hours beforehand never seems to dull the actual experience. Seeing the landscape firsthand *always* stirs the explorer in me.

Solo trips are inspirational for some, but friendship continues to be the cornerstone of the tramping experience. In an environment stripped of urban 'bunk', friendships form without artifice. At other times friendship is heightened by adversity. As Shaun and I continued our epic up the Otoko we were separated for an hour or so. Looking back there was no real problem in this. We both knew where we were going, we both had a map and compass and both of us love the moments of solitude that can be had in the hills. Yet when we reunited further up the valley, our friendship had never seemed so important.

Finally, tramping seems to offer a greater chance of experiencing moments that engrave themselves in our minds, even more than words or photographs – they could be an event or happening that turns around a difficult day; a moment that presents itself so strongly it becomes *the* memory.

One of these occurred for me at Daleys Flat in the Dart Valley after a cold wet day's tramping. The evening turned out sunny and I found a spot to sit among some beech trees. In the warmth I was beginning to forget how damp and chilled I'd been earlier in the day, when a bush robin hopped up and began to check me out from all angles. Deciding I was no threat, the robin hopped onto my bare feet and began to feast on the sandflies gathering on my longjohns. I doubt I will ever adequately find the words to describe the sensation of its spindly feet on my skin; there was certainly no possibility or desire to bring a camera into the moment. That is the way with many such instances. They may be fleeting, yet they feed the memories that make the hard slog worthwhile, inspiring us to head back into the hills time and again.

Rob Brown

Evening light on the Tararua Peaks (RB).

THE TARARUA PEAKS

The traditional home of tramping

In the early part of the twentieth century, much of New Zealand was still wild and largely unexplored. Those heading off into the hills faced formidable barriers; a lack of tracks and huts, equipment which was woefully substandard for mountain weather, as well as access and transport limitations. It was not until the formation of clubs that tramping started to become a more common pastime, and in 1919 New Zealand's first tramping club was named after a series of mountains just north of Wellington – the Tararuas.

Clubs attracted like-minded people and provided a chance for novices to learn from more experienced members, a process which still continues. In the early days, people like Fred Vosseler, Edwin Boyd-Wilson and Sam McIntosh were all club stalwarts who helped move the experience of wild country from the exclusive domain of hardy explorers into the grasp of everyday people. A quick glance at the Tararua map reveals that their contribution to the culture of tramping has been appropriately remembered, even if it was just the naming of a small bump or knoll on a ridge.

Over the years, clubs have been instrumental in establishing a dense network of tracks and huts in the range, firstly by the Tararua Tramping Club and then latterly by some of the other local clubs such as the Wellington Tramping and Mountaineering Club and the Hutt Valley Tramping Club. Clubs became adept at organising trips. More often than not transport to the start of the trip would

be on the back of a truck and trampers would be bounced along rutted roads into the hills for weekend excursions. Otaki Forks, inland from the township of Otaki, became a focal point for many of these trips, and here begins one of the classic North Island tramps – a traverse of the Tararua Peaks.

Starting from the prominent river junction at Otaki Forks, a well-gravelled track climbs steadily through bracken scrub before entering the forest. The three hour climb to Field Hut is not difficult, but try to imagine the backbreaking effort of lugging an iron water tank up here. In 1924, Fred Vosseler and Bill Denton did just this as the load was too awkward even for pack horses to carry it up to the newly built hut. Commissioned by the Tararua Tramping Club, the hut was built by Joe Gibbs using timber pit sawn on site and horses to carry the corrugated iron for the cladding.

Having considerably lighter packs than the early hut builders you are able to appreciate rather than curse the forest, which is at first dominated by dense groves of kamahi (*Weinmannia racemosa*), sprouting upwards like pitchforks. Each time gales push one kamahi over, new branches sprout from the fallen trunk, resulting in dense thickets. Further up are moss-encrusted beech and totara trees and on the forest floor the ubiquitous crown fern (*Blechnum discolor*). At the edge of the bush on a flat shelf hacked from the ridge is Field Hut. This historic shelter (the second oldest surviving hut in the Tararuas) serves as a lunch stop, or even a place for the night if

Hurrying to Field Hut for a hot brew (RB).

Kime Hut in early winter (SB).

you've walked in late on a Friday evening. Recently, the Tararua Tramping Club installed a series of photographs and information panels to commemorate the history of the hut.

Above Field Hut, the forest merges into subalpine scrub. The Tararuas have ill-defined bushlines and instead boast a large band of tough, woody-stemmed plants known (not so affectionately) as scrub. The dominant plant here is leatherwood (*Olearia colensoi*), an exceptionally resilient tree daisy with leaves like cowhide and a shape somewhere between a wire brush and a bonsai tree. Trampers have been known to curse its existence when forced to travel through it in untracked terrain as the stout branches are too dense to crawl under and just weak enough to defy climbing over. Fortunately, a well-defined track leads through the thick subalpine band to the tussock tops, and you can enjoy the diverse array of plants without needing to battle them.

Unlike many South Island trips, travel in the Tararuas is largely on the tops, which is one of the range's best features. On a fine day, views unfold of ridges rising like rows of ship prows right out to Kapiti Island off the coast. More often, however, the Tararua Ranges are subject to savage winds and thick cloud, and this has earned them a terrible reputation for bad weather. Statistics do nothing to dispel the reputation; on the tops storm conditions are experienced for an average of 200 days per year. In tramping terminology, such weather is referred to as murk or crud, and blamed on the most

Sunrise on the main Tararua Range from Hut Mound (SB).

13

fickle of deities, the weather god Huey. Huey has an evil sense of humour and likes nothing better than smothering trampers in the worst of weather, tempting them with just enough snippets of blue sky only to later dash any hopes of a clearance.

Even on one of Huey's particularly nasty days, there are no

Ascending the chain ladder between the Tararua Peaks (SB).

problems reaching Kime Hut on a track with liberal snow poles placed at short, mist-defying intervals. Situated in a partially sheltered tussock bowl, the twenty-four bunk hut is actually the second version, built in 1978, well after the previous one fell into disrepair. During the 1930s, the original Kime Hut had its own ski field, but less reliable snow in later years saw the demise of skiing. However, with a high ceiling, no mattresses or wood stove, the present Kime Hut can still be very cold in winter.

The route north towards the Tararua Peaks requires backtracking a short distance to Bridge Peak, where a pole marks the start of the descent on to the main Tararua Range. From here the tramping is along a vague ridge route, with a progression of sharp climbs and drops negotiating a series of tussock knolls between 1,100 and 1,400 metres in height, each named after some of the early trampers who explored the area in the 1930s. There is the occasional cairn and a fairly well-defined route worn over the years by trampers' boots, but misty conditions may require navigation with a compass. Even if you're lucky enough to have a clear day, there's likely to be a brisk wind whipping in from the coast.

Walking in a strong wind often requires a compensatory lean, with shorter strides to avoid overbalancing in the irregular gusts. While traversing Vosseler, my coat flapped wildly and the gusts sometimes snatched the breath from my lungs. The incessant westerly helped push us up the climbs, the continual buffeting lending our movements a certain urgency, as if the wind's energy was being blown into us. Suddenly, where the route dropped abruptly to the lee side of the ridge, the wind vanished. Having got used to the resistance, I stumbled off balance, while my coat's movements eased to gentle rustling. On the ridge crest above I could see the wind-whipped tussocks, but five metres to the lee we walked in a calm, quiet world where every breath could be heard.

After passing the summit of McIntosh, the silhouettes of the Tararua Peaks loom ahead, and invariably cloud adds to the alarming profile of their sharp cones. This section is the crux of the route, with a challenging traverse that requires a good head for heights. In

March 1930, eight young men from the Tararua Tramping Club pioneered the route over the Tararua Peaks after an earlier defeat. On the first trip they'd been thwarted by the impressive gulch lying between the peaks of Tunui and Tuiti. Better prepared on their second attempt, they negotiated the notch using a rope in the same place where a chain ladder now allows trampers a safe descent. Beyond the ladder is a narrow sidle around the base of Tunui, the second cone-shaped peak, and a series of sharp climbs and rock scrambles leads the short distance to Maungahuka Hut.

Maungahuka Hut is positioned in a sheltered hollow beside a tarn on tussock tops and is one of the best spots in the Tararua Range. On a good day the views stretch from the Pacific Ocean to the Tasman Sea, with the main range unfolding into the distance ahead. Such scenes are easily captured on film, but it is more difficult to record the sounds of the high country, "the rattle of scree, the thump of falling rock, ... a nor'wester screeching..." as poet Brian Turner writes. Inside the hut after dusk other sounds predominate; the purr of the burner, the spatter of a flickering candle and the creak of timbers as night cools the shelter.

After a night at Maungahuka Hut, the third day involves a long traverse of exposed tops leading eventually to Anderson Memorial Hut. If the clouds part there are fine views over two of the most impressive gorges in the Tararuas; the Otaki to the west, and the Waiohine to the east. However, when rain lashes in at horizontal angles threatening to work its cold fingers up under your coat, travel on the ridge is more a case of pulling the balaclava low, tightening the pack straps and forging on with your head down. This sort of traditional Tararua weather may be unpleasant, but it is certainly good for improving the navigation skills and stamina necessary for harder wilderness trips.

The notorious Tararua murk is tempered by rugged and magnificent scenery, and it is this combination which often causes trampers to have a love-hate relationship with the range. One writer and historian, John Pascoe, aptly described this relationship in his book *Land Uplifted High*: "For sheer miserable monotony of con-

tour, rigour of weather, and bleakness of outlook it is hard to beat the Tararuas. They are to Wellington trampers what oatmeal is to Scottish people; dull solid fare which gives them staple virtues."

If the conditions are rough, it may indeed be with some relief that you pass over Kahiwiroa and, after a further kilometre, reach

Maungahuka Hut (SB).

the shelter of the forest. This section has a 'Lord of the Rings' ambience and is the sort of place you might expect an elf or goblin to appear. Because of the altitude, the tree limbs are twisted at arthritic angles and moss hangs in great dripping clumps from every surface. If there's mist about, the poor visibility reduces distant trees to a colourless grey, with only the foreground retaining any shades of green.

After walking through this almost monochrome world, the orange roof of Anderson Memorial Hut comes as a bold finish to the day. In 1946, this hut became the first to be airlifted into the ranges, with the prefabricated sections parachuted onto site by pilot Oliver Anderson (who was tragically later killed on a flight in Fiordland).

Past this hut are some wonderful tussock tops, an occasional tarn and a steady rise to Junction Knob, appropriately named, as it

Moss covered silver beech forest near Anderson Memorial Hut (SB).

Moving along the main ridge near Simpson (SB).

is here you leave the main range and begin the forested descent into the Otaki River. Once down in the valley, a long swingbridge crosses the Otaki River, affording a giddy view of the current below. Suspended high above on the wire structure is a great position from which to watch the roar of the torrid, muddy waters when the Otaki is in one of its frequent floods.

Built in 1990 to replace the original and situated beside the river, Waitewaewae Hut is by far the largest and most comfortable on the trip. There are places to camp not far from the hut, and at weekends the area is usually a hum of activity with sometimes large groups of trampers enjoying the river and forest. In the early days of the Tararua Tramping Club, large parties of thirty to forty peo-

ple were not unheard of, and tramping must have been a festive occasion. Imagine the lumpy stews concocted in cauldron-like billies over the camp fire to feed groups of this size. Later in the evening, as night fell around the embers, tramper-lore recalls these parties erupting into raucous songs of sometimes dubious lyrics.

The last day is spent entirely sheltered in forest, with a climb over a swampy plateau followed by a descent down Saddle Creek to Waitatapia Stream. Beyond Saddle Creek, the track emerges onto an old tramline, dating back to the 1930s when timber (mainly rimu) was hauled out to Corrigan's Mill near Otaki Forks. In many places the rusting iron tracks are still in place, and the well benched gradient is a delight to follow. Beside the track in one section is an

Ridgeline near Anderson Memorial Hut (SB).

old steam log-hauler, in remarkable condition, making an interesting reminder of the logging days.

When the mill was still in operation the rapidly diminishing forest stirred people, many of them trampers, to lobby the government for protection of the Tararua forests. There were even unsuccessful proposals for a Tararua National Park in 1937, and again in 1952, but two years later the New Zealand Forest Service, who managed the area, decided to instead create the first Forest Park.

National Park legislation was too restrictive for the Forest Service's multiple use concept, which embraced production as well as protection. Forest Parks were created to protect forested catchments and encourage recreation, but they also allowed some areas to be planted in exotic trees for timber. Since the formation of the Department of Conservation in 1987, however, New Zealand's nine-teen Forest Parks have become part of the conservation estate and no longer allow uses inappropriate to conservation.

Despite the removal of the rimu, the last few hours of the tramp pass through forest with a pleasant diversity of trees, the dominant varieties being beech, kamahi, hinau, mahoe and rewa-rewa. Beneath the canopy, tangles of supplejack and tall tree ferns shut out the light, giving the forest a cool, damp atmosphere. If, after five days of foul weather, you have, as John Pascoe did, formed unfavourable first impressions of the Tararuas, remember that the range can be painfully shy in revealing the rugged charm of its peaks; even Pascoe had to concede that the park offers a "variety of bush and river scenery just as pleasant as the beauty of the Maori names it compassed."

Shaun Barnett

THE TARARUA PEAKS
Tararua Forest Park

Length: 46 kilometres.
Time required: 4–5 days.
Nearest town: Otaki.
Best time to walk track: October to May.
Fitness: Good fitness required.
Map (1:50,000): S26 Carterton.

Information: Department of Conservation, PO Box 5086, Wellington. Phone: 04 472 5821. Fax: 04 499 0077.
Department of Conservation, PO Box 141, Waikanae. Phone: 04 293 2191. Fax: 04 293 6020. Otaki Base Phone: 06 364 3111.

A classic Tararua trip with a mixture of bush ridges, open tops and valley travel. The track from Otaki Forks to Kime Hut is well marked and although exposed, should not present well-equipped trampers with any difficulties. However, between Bridge Peak and Shoulder Knob travel is on an exposed, unmarked route requiring good navigation skills in bad weather. One section (around the Tararua Peaks themselves) negotiates a chain ladder and some rock steps. Parties with concerns about the steepness would be better to do the trip in reverse, giving an ascent (rather than descent) of the ladder. From Waitewaewae Hut the track is well marked and sheltered in the forest.

The weather is notoriously unpredictable and parties should always be well-equipped with warm clothing and wet weather gear. Winter trips are possible, but a serious undertaking when snow covers the tops. A Department of Conservation Annual Hut Pass covers fees for all of the huts, but carry a sleeping mat as there are no mattresses at either Kime or Field Huts. Camping is limited, but possible at Waitewaewae and Kime.

Access to the round trip begins and ends at Otaki Forks, inland from Otaki township. At the forks there is a carpark, ranger's house and emergency phone.

Approximate track times:
Otaki Forks to Kime Hut (35 bunks): 11 kilometres, 4–6 hours.
Kime Hut to Maungahuka Hut (6 bunks): 8 kilometres, 4–5 hours.
Maungahuka Hut to Anderson Memorial Hut (6 bunks): 9 kilometres, 6–7 hours.
Anderson Memorial Hut to Waitewaewae Hut (30 bunks): 8 kilometres, 3–4 hours.
Waitewaewae Hut to Otaki Forks: 10 kilometres, 4–5 hours.

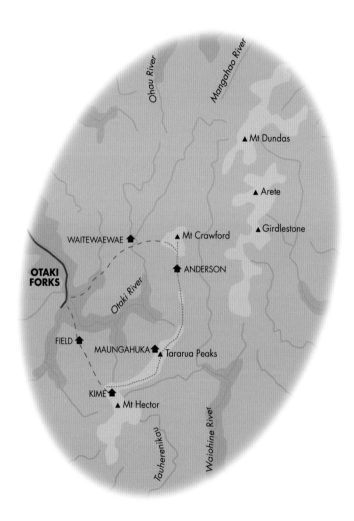

‧‧‧‧‧‧‧ Rivers	Over 1550 m	300–1550 m	0–300 m
—— Main roads	·········· Routes	⬆ Huts	⚫ Rock bivvy
– – – Walking tracks	▲ Mountains	) (Saddles	

FIORDLAND NATIONAL PARK
THE HOLLYFORD
No place for a road

The standard Hollyford tramp follows the meandering course of the Hollyford River between Martins Bay on the west coast and the road end near Gunns Camp in the Hollyford Valley. The Hollyford Track stays below the bushline as it journeys between these two points, and has an unfair reputation amongst hardier trampers as a boring walk in the forest with no views. Such a blinkered judgment is perhaps locked into the western concept of view as meaning looking down on things or at least out across a sweeping vista. The Hollyford provides the opportunity to break out of this paradigm by offering breathtaking views in a skyward direction, and is also an ideal adventure for anyone with an aversion to going uphill!

While light aircraft can be used to reach the starting point at Martins Bay, a pleasant addition to the standard tramp is to fly slightly further north to Big Bay and take an extra day walking the spectacular coastline south to the mouth of the Hollyford River. A twenty minute flight to the low tide landing strip on the beach at Big Bay offers a grand but removed perspective on the landscape you are about to enter. The overwhelming impression of this aerial view is of how dramatically water, in both solid and liquid forms, has shaped the land. To the south, the form of the Darran Mountains reflects the way ice, wind and rain have conspired to create an inhospitable topography. Draining the catchments of these great peaks, the rivers and creeks, which obviously see their fair share of floods, cut jagged paths through lush green forest as they battle to find the easiest paths to the Hollyford.

With westerly gusts buffeting the aircraft, landing at Big Bay can be a little unsettling, especially with the knowledge that the area has not been without its aeronautical drama. On 30 December 1936, a tourist flight *en route* to Franz Josef ditched in the bay while approaching the beach to deliver a passenger. A tramping party, led by local guide and land-owner Davy Gunn, watched helplessly as the drama unfolded, and then set about trying to rescue the occupants. One person was dead, but four survivors were dragged ashore in varying states of injury and shock. At seven in the evening, Davy Gunn set off on a nonstop dash to raise the alarm; riding his horse around the coast, rowing 15 kilometres up Lake McKerrow and then walking 40 kilometres to the nearest phone at Hollyford Camp – a marathon twenty-one hours of hard physical travel which saved four lives. In essence, it is the route of Gunn's dash that this tramp follows, though at a more sedate pace over six days!

Hidden behind sand dunes south of the main cluster of whitebaiters' cribs is the Department of Conservation's Big Bay Hut. Its log book is full of stories of those who, with season and weather permitting, have taken a purist's approach to Big Bay by walking for three to five days (and sometimes longer!) via the Hollyford and Pyke valleys. While some had sauntered up the route in fine weather and had a relatively enjoyable time, most had been caught by one of the frequent weather changes that afflict the area,

(Left) Early morning at Big Bay (RB).
(Above) Fiordland crested penguin, Long Point (SB).

Dawn at the mouth of the Hollyford River (SB).

and by some accounts almost didn't make it to the bay.

Big Bay has a similar ambience to the wild beaches of Stewart Island. However, unlike Stewart Island, Big Bay is largely free of the refuse turfed off fishing boats with depressing regularity. There is something almost spiritual about walking along a wild, unlittered section of coastline where forest runs right down to the sea and stretched before you is a beach without footprints. Despite the constant crash of breakers, such beaches are strangely peaceful and remind me of an old Japanese proverb: 'the sound of the sea and the sound of the heart are the same'.

At the southern end of Big Bay beach I came across a pair of New Zealand dotterels (*Charadrius obscurus*) staunchly defending their nest by faking a broken wing and moving away from their exposed eggs. Perturbed that I hadn't fallen for their ruse (how were they to know I'd read about their tricks in a book!), they flew back towards me to regain my attention. I stood still and scanned the shells, flotsam, logs and clumps of pingao because I knew from the frantic charade going on just 5 metres away that I must have inadvertently strayed very close to their nest. I moved on after about a minute, taking extreme care placing my feet, knowing that my eyesight had already been defeated by the superior camouflage of the dotterels' eggs.

It is never much fun shouldering a pack at the start of a long trip, but setting out from Big Bay the following morning I quickly realised one of the fundamental truths of flying to the start of any tramp – no matter how hard you try not to take too much food and equipment, you always take too much food and equipment. Before the trip I'd had the bright idea of taking a fishing rod in the hope of living from the spoils of sea and river and cutting down on food. Not surprisingly, my companions were unimpressed and I soon found myself staggering not only under the load of camera and fishing gear but also the food for my designated cooking nights. As it turned out, their lack of regard for my fishing skills was well founded! I would have done well to have read Davy Gunn's stern advice to his tramping clients: "Try to keep your pack below twenty

Hokuri Hut (RB).

pounds as you will find a multitude of possessions a weariness to the flesh."

As is often the case with tramping, the initial shock of your heavy pack subsides once you get into a plodding rhythm of movement fuelled by healthy gasps of clean air. It takes about five hours of this steady locomotion along gravel beaches and over conglomerate boulders to reach Long Point, from where you can look for the first time across the impressive sweep of Martins Bay.

Long Point is a breeding area for New Zealand fur seals (*Arctocephalus forsteri*) and Fiordland crested penguins (*Eudyptes pachyrhynchus*), so allowing time here is a must for those hoping to observe these animals at close quarters. I spent an afternoon at the point sitting not far from a mother seal and her young pup which was pestering her for milk. When there was no milk left the pup was gently pushed away and the mother folded her flippers over her teats. For the next hour she quietly rebuffed its endearingly persistent efforts to nuzzle back in for more milk, until the pup eventually gave up, stretched out over her back and accepted that it was, perhaps, full enough.

As the sun sank behind the clouds of an approaching front, we watched seal pups frolic and chase each other amongst pools and boulders. Meanwhile, following their own plan at this time of the day, increasing numbers of Fiordland crested penguins were returning from the sea. Completely unperturbed by the presence of the seals and only slightly so by the three humans on their patch, they preened themselves for a time, then hopped and waddled over the boulders into the protective tangle of kiekie on the bush edge where nest, mate and hungry chicks awaited.

Half an hour from Long Point, Martins Bay Hut is tucked inside coastal forest opposite the Holly-ford River mouth, and is a cosy place to get the fire going, make a cup of tea and reflect on the day's walking. The atmosphere is special enough to warrant an extra day here before heading inland along the Hollyford Track proper.

Big Bay (SB).

The southern side of Martins Bay was, for many years, a significant Maori canoe-building settlement, the large rimu (*Dacrydium cupressinum*) trees in the area being especially suited for this purpose. When Europeans came to Martins Bay, or Kotuku as it was known to local Maori, it was all but deserted. In residence was an old chief, Tutoko, and his wife and two daughters. Fiordland's highest peak now bears his name, while his daughters are remembered by their European names in the Sara and May Hills either side of the bay.

As the track penetrates inland, the sound of the ocean fades to a distant hum and is replaced by the rustle of wind in the trees. The trail follows a deep, wide stretch of the Hollyford River below Lake McKerrow and, after a short stroll through towering forest, emerges onto the shores of the lake itself. At one time this large body of water would have been the area's northernmost fiord, but over time soil and sand have sealed the entrance creating the lake. Tests have revealed that a salty layer still exists beneath the overlying fresh water. For nearly two hours the track is along the gravel shore and, if you are lucky enough, you will see pods of dolphins cruising close by. It's thought that they swim up the Holly-ford into the lake for a sort of therapeutic bath; the fresh water killing any parasites that have accumulated on their skin at sea.

Kowhai are prolific along the forest fringe here, and in early spring numerous tui and bellbirds flock to feed on nectar. During this time, the Department of Conservation traps stoats to allow the birds to feed without being attacked. Infestations of introduced predators have accelerated in the last ten years, and the local residents have noticed a marked drop in bird populations. That the birdlife still appears in good numbers to a city dweller like myself hints at how seriously the urban environment erodes expectations.

Just before Hokuri Hut, the track curves around a crescent-shaped bay to the site of the abandoned settlement of Jamestown. Jamestown, founded in 1870, was named after the Superintendent of Otago, James Macandrew, who urged it into being as part of a bold scheme to establish a western port at Martins Bay. It was during a period when considerable money was being invested in infrastructural projects such as ports, roads and settlements, but in places like Fiordland the realities of climate, terrain and isolation could easily overwhelm grand schemes. After nine years of

Fallen trees on the banks of the Hollyford River (SB).

Crossing a small stream on the Demon Trail (SB).

hardship and suffering, not to mention the failure to build a road to the settlement, Jamestown was abandoned, though people continued to live in the area. The advent of tourism has enabled a small number (fluctuating between ten and twenty) to take up the private land around Jamestown and call this part of the world home.

Of all the area's settlers, Daniel McKenzie made the best go of it and stayed until about 1903, farming the grassy flats at the southern end of Martins Bay. Incredibly, he used to drive his stock 250 kilometres along the Hollyford Track, over the Divide into the Greenstone Valley, along the Mavora Trail, and, eventually, to the saleyards at Mossburn. You will appreciate what a monumental effort in stock driving this must have been when you set out from Hokuri Hut along the Demon Trail. As a tramping route, the Demon Trail section of the Hollyford is not actually *that* bad, but as with most sidling tracks it combines a fair bit of weaving in and out of gullies with a generous helping of up and down.

A curious by-product of the settler era that still persists today is the proposal to link Haast and Milford Sound by a road via the Hollyford. A report produced after a possible route was surveyed in 1864 concluded that a road was both impractical and not possible with the technology of the day. But every few years the idea resurfaces and public money is lavished on a feasibility study. Such a road would split this wilderness in two and in every way destroy the integrity of the landscape. The charm of places like the Hollyford is derived from being able to take your time and appreciate the damp smells of the forest, the birds, the rain on your face and feel the ground beneath your feet as you walk.

After a few more hours of walking, where the main highlights are likely to be the intermittent calls of kaka and kakariki, Demon Trail Hut is reached at a pleasant point halfway along the Demon Trail. From here comes another relaxing day's walk through more mixed beech and rimu forest to Alabaster Hut. Two hours beyond Demon Trail Hut, the long sidle of Lake McKerrow is completed when the track arrives on the banks of the Hollyford. The flow of water here is breathtaking and due largely to the contribution of

Forest interior near the junction of the Pyke and Hollyford Rivers (RB).

Female fur seal and pup, Long Point (RB).

another voluminous river, the Pyke, which gathers its water from a huge catchment on the edge of the Red Hills in the southern part of the Olivine Wilderness Area. These waters are eventually fed into Lake Alabaster and enter the Hollyford below the Pyke River swingbridge. Fifteen minutes upstream of the bridge, Alabaster Hut provides cosy lodgings and is well used by fishermen, hunters and trampers alike.

On the final morning of the tramp, the first thing you notice is the change in the standard of the track. Wide and benched, the path leads you through one of the last great areas of lowland beech and rimu forest in the country. The trees here are majestic in a way that only very large living things can be. Beneath a pretty waterfall, a bridge is crossed before the track heads up the only short climb of the tramp to Little Homer Saddle. Soon after the crossing the track curves around to a sensational viewpoint. Mt Tutoko (2,746 metres) is the highest mountain in Fiordland National Park and in fine weather its icy summit is visible from many parts of the Hollyford. Such is the scale of Tutoko from this angle that I suspect even the most hardened mountaineers would be left looking skywards with mouths slightly ajar and eyes glazed in bewilderment. Other peaks in New Zealand may have greater heights next to their names but no other mountain in the Southern Alps looks as impregnable and intimidating. It was a sight that literally took my breath away, and I sat at this spot for close to an hour – with plenty of daylight and just a few hours walking to go there was no need to finish the tramp too hastily.

Rob Brown

THE HOLLYFORD TRACK

Fiordland National Park

Length: 66 kilometres (including Big Bay to Martins Bay).
Time required: 6 days.
Nearest town: Te Anau.
Best time to walk track: All year round.
Fitness: Moderate fitness required.
Maps (1:50,000): D40 Milford, D38 Lake McKerrow.

The Hollyford is a lowland journey with a highest point of 152 metres (Little Homer Saddle) and is the only major track in Fiordland which can be walked all year round. The major flood-prone creeks are bridged and crossable in all but the worst weather.

There are two ways to reach Big Bay. The easiest is to charter one of the air services which runs small Cessna planes in the Fiordland area. Both Air Fiordland and Hollyford Walks operate from the Hollyford strip and land on the beach at Big Bay. For the more hardy, you can walk to Big Bay via the Pyke River Valley. This route involves walking into Alabaster Hut on the Hollyford Track and then heading up the Pyke on an old, unmaintained route to Lake Wilmot and from here crossing over to Big Bay. This is definitely a remote experience area, and it takes three to five long hard days to reach Big Bay from the Hollyford road end. Most of the Pyke River valley is prone to flooding, and none of the rivers are bridged. Parties have gotten into trouble on this route in heavy rain.

A third option for trampers just wanting to reach Martins Bay is to simply walk in from and back out to the Hollyford road end. An option to shorten the return journey is to charter the jet boat to get back up Lake McKerrow. This can be booked with the Martins Bay Lodge and avoids repeating the two days on the Demon Trail. All huts are covered by the Department of Conservation's Annual Hut Pass and have wood burners for heating. There are few suitable places to camp.

Approximate track times:
Big Bay Hut (9 bunks) **to Martins Bay Hut** (4 platforms, equal to 16–18 bunks): 15 kilometres, 5–6 hours.
Martins Bay Hut to Hokuri Hut (2 platforms, equal to 12–14 bunks): 9.5 kilometres, 3.5–4.5 hours.
Hokuri Hut to Demon Trail Hut (12 bunks): 11.5 kilometres, 5–6 hours.
Demon Trail Hut to Alabaster Hut (2 platforms, equal to 12–14 bunks): 12 kilometres, 5–6 hours.
Alabaster Hut to Hidden Falls Hut (2 platforms, equal to 12-14 bunks): 10 kilometres, 3-4 hours.
Hidden Falls Hut to Hollyford road end: 8 kilometres, 2–3 hours.

Information: Department of Conservation, Lake Front Drive, PO Box 29, Te Anau. Phone: 03 249 7924. Fax: 03 249 7613. Air Fiordland, 70 Town Centre, Te Anau. Phone: 03 249 7505. Fax: 03 249 7080. Hollyford Valley Walk Ltd, PO Box 360, Queenstown. Freephone: 0800 832 226. Fax: 03 442 3761.

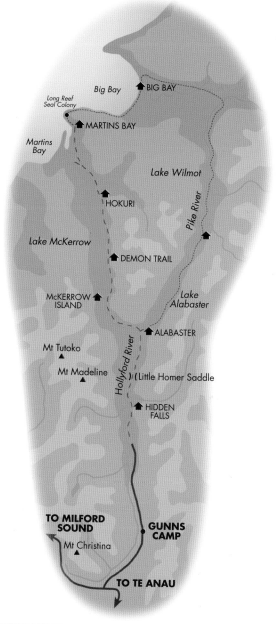

	Rivers		Over 1550 m		300–1550 m		0–300 m
	Main roads		Routes	▲	Huts		Rock bivvy
	Walking tracks	▲	Mountains	)(	Saddles		

NELSON LAKES TO LEWIS PASS

Gentle mountain country

In the mountains of Nelson Lakes National Park, the Main Divide of the Southern Alps splits into a series of ridges like the bones of a splayed hand. Between these long ridges are several curved valleys bearing the distinct imprint of past glacial action. Although the ice ages may have left the mountains here with slightly less spectacular features than those further south, the compensation lies in country of a gradient ideal for trampers. In summer, none of the passes require mountaineering skills, tracks are well defined and the climate gentler than most of the mountain regions further west or south. A traverse of the park's entire length, from St Arnaud to Lewis Pass, can be accomplished in as little as a week using the generous number of huts along most of the route.

During the end of the last ice age, melt water from receding glaciers formed the park's two largest lakes, Rotoroa and Rotoiti. The trip begins at Lake Rotoiti, the smaller of the two, and here there is a choice of routes. Both Speargrass Stream or the Travers Valley and Saddle lead over to the Sabine Valley and the route south, but a personal favourite is the route over Mt Robert along Robert Ridge, on the northern side of Lake Rotoiti. Despite its steep gradient, the zigzag track at the start of Robert Ridge is one of the park's most popular walks, undoubtedly for its views. In every direction, mountains recede into rippled folds; the clean, sharp bushline, so characteristic of Nelson Lakes, giving way to countless summits. A solid day on the tops following

a poled route leads past a small club ski field and over a series of knolls, arriving finally at Lake Angelus.

The ragged lake fills a cirque basin, with the nearby hut built on a tussock mound under the imposing cone of Mt Angelus. Golden tussock mingles with patches of scree, and in summer, when gentians, buttercups and daisies are in flower, the area is a botanist's delight. Alpine regions are at their best on a warm day when it's possible to laze between tussocks and watch the grasshoppers leap about with kamikaze abandon. The best place to do just this is at nearby Hinapouri Tarn, a spectacular little lake that seems to change hue as the sun arches across the sky. Lying here in the sun and gazing at the view brought to mind a description by Katherine Mansfield of a day "so clear, so silent, so still, you [could] almost feel the earth itself [had] stopped in astonishment at its own beauty."

The large Angelus Hut lies at the junction of several tracks and in summer may be close to full with arrivals from Mt Robert and the Travers and Sabine Valleys. The route south leads over Mt Cedric before dropping down to where the Sabine River merges into Lake Rotoroa. From the tussock slopes of Mt Cedric, the oblong lake tapers away like a pounamu (greenstone) pendant. There is a sense of being on a shoulder directly above the water, and you quickly realise the descent will be very steep. But tree trunks form convenient handholds to brake the plunge until finally the forest

(Left) Lake Rotoroa (RB).
(Above) Blue Lake Hut (SB).

fans onto the quiet lake edge near Sabine Hut.

Once I'd claimed a bunk and unpacked my gear, I slipped down to the jetty where I watched woodsmoke from the hut's fire curl and waft like a grey scarf over the perfectly still lake. Absorbed by the beauty and tranquillity of places like this, I sometimes find myself entering an almost meditative state where my thoughts fill with the present, and everyday concerns peel away. Such moments might be fleeting, lasting only until the persistent nip of sandflies or the evening's chill take me back inside, but they are nevertheless one of the great sources of pleasure during a tramp.

Nelson Lakes National Park comprises five major valleys – the D'Urville, Sabine, Travers, Matakitaki and Glenroy. All are dominated by beech forests, which form an essential element of the park's beauty.

The route up the Sabine wanders below tall, mature beech forest with a grand spaciousness in its understorey. In beech forests, the absence of dense tangles of podocarp and broadleaf trees is often made up for by mosses, fungi and lichens, and the Sabine Valley is no exception. In places the moss rides thickly up the tree trunks like debris left by an outgoing tide. Often hidden beneath these mossy carpets are large boulders deposited not by a great unleashing force such as a landslide, but by the subtle tug of gravity.

Ridgeline above Lake Angelus (Scott Freeman).

Hinapouri Tarn (RB).

This is how it is for much of the way mountain landscapes are shaped. Occasional bursts of energy like earthquakes can vastly alter landscapes in a matter of minutes, but it is the ever-active forces of gravity, glaciation, tectonic uplift, water erosion and weathering that craft the land over long periods of time, moving mountains literally rock by rock.

The forests of Nelson Lakes are home to good populations of South Island robins (*Petroica australis australis*), and when one perches on your boot and looks at you with a quizzical sideways

South Island robin (SB).

glance, its chumminess seems more than mere interest in the insects you have attracted. Even after you carry on up the track, a robin will often follow you for a distance, hopping spryly on legs as thin as tooth picks.

Halfway up the Sabine Valley, the river forks and the track continues up the banks of the west branch. The gradient steepens and one of the classic landscapes of Nelson Lakes unfolds – a bold, cascading river flanked by mountain beech forest and framed by craggy summits. Eventually, the steady stream-side climb eases, and a short section of forest leads to Blue Lake Hut. Here, near the

head of the West Sabine, is a lake of exceptional beauty, and one of the trip's highlights. Blue Lake is certainly blue, but the name does little justice to the exquisite shade of blue-green that deepens as the lake gets deeper. It is one of those places that changes mood and colour depending from where you view it. From its edge it mirrors the forested shore in a perfect but subdued reflection, while from above it appears like a bold turquoise jewel embedded in the green and gold of the valley.

The next stage, crossing from Blue Lake to the Waiau Valley, is long and tiring, but what a day! – almost all above the bushline, past mountain lakes, over a high alpine pass and down into the edge of Canterbury. Beyond Blue Lake lies the much larger Lake Constance trapped behind an extensive moraine wall. Following the skyline leads your eye from the eastern ridge of Mt Mahanga to the low point of Waiau Pass. At nearly 1,900 metres, Waiau is amongst the highest of Nelson Lakes' passes and is approached first with a high sidle around Lake Constance to avoid bluffs.

From the head of the lake, a poled route edges its way up steep scree slopes onto the pass where a whole new vista of mountains opens out. Divided by the curl of the upper Waiau River are the Spenser Mountains to the west, with the peaks of the St James Range to the east. The sharp descent from Waiau Pass demands care on the loose ground underfoot. After picking your way down rock gullies and wending around cliffs, the first trickle of the Waiau River is finally reached.

From here it's possible to continue out through the St James Station to the St James Walkway, but if the weather holds, a much more challenging alternative lies in using two passes over the Spenser Mountains. We opted for this harder route as the forested valleys make for much more pleasant surroundings than the cattle flats of the station.

The Spenser Mountains mark the boundary between Nelson Lakes National Park to the west and the St James Station to the east. They were named by William Travers, an Irish emigrant who, with Christopher Maling, reached the Waiau Valley in 1860 after travelling from the Clarence Valley in the east. Travers bestowed the glistening summits with the name of his favourite poet, the Englishman Edmund Spenser. One of the mountains bears the name of Spenser's epic poem, *The Faerie Queene*, and other peak names, including Gloriana, Una and Duessa, are borrowed from characters in the verse.

The first pass over the Spenser Mountains requires a climb to Lake Thompson at the source of the Waiau. At 1,400 metres, Lake Thompson provides an idyllic if chilly camp site, surrounded by the sharp outline of the Spenser Mountains. A quick ascent onto Thompson Pass a short distance above the lake follows in the morning. Because the poled route has now finished and cairns are few, there's likely to be some apprehension about the route. Don't be tempted, as we were, to drop straight from the pass down an obvious scree gut – it ends in bluffs. Instead, traverse the ridge running south-east, and sidle into the head of a large alpine basin at the head of the D'Urville River. Here you cross an unmarked pass, sometimes referred to as the Upper D'Urville Pass, which leads from the western side of this basin into the head of the East Matakitaki Valley.

The map depicts the Matakitaki with two long branches like enormous crab pincers probing into the western slopes of the Spensers. Both branches have a delicious remoteness and isolation not felt so keenly in the more popular northern valleys of Nelson Lakes. The Matakitaki huts are small, classic New Zealand Forest Service constructions, which are the ultimate in simple, functional design – open fires, mattressed bunks, a cooking bench and not much else.

The East Matakitaki curls through a series of tussock flats with forest crowding in on its flanks and distant mountains rising in clean geometric shapes beyond. Further down valley, the east and west branches merge and close into a narrow gorge near the junction. Here, a three-wire bridge crosses the chasm. Three-wire bridges provide a simple means of crossing rivers, but require more caution than a conventional swingbridge. One with a sagging cen-

Sabine River below Blue Lake (RB).

tral wire can be quite unnerving, and I've crossed a few that have left me lurching midway like an off-balance trapeze artist. At maximum stretch it's very difficult to maintain a dignified air, especially when you're all too aware of the drop below. Fortunately, the one leading to Bobs Hut is taut and safe.

Bobs Hut sits in an expansive tussock clearing at the culmination of numerous bush ridges sweeping down the mountains like the buttresses of a tree. Despite having visited it four times, each trip has been a unique experience, partly due to season, but largely

Heading down the East Matakitaki River (SB).

because of my travelling companions. By this stage any annoying habits will be plainly evident. Perhaps someone has a bunk-rattling snore combined with an uncanny ability to get to sleep first. But to compensate they might bring you a steaming hot drink just when your energy is low at the end of the day. Mountains create a setting where big topics can be raised and conversations can flow like the rivers. At other times, when faced with scenes of unspeakable beauty, talk lapses into companionable silences.

From Bobs Hut the Spenser Mountains are crossed one last time via an unnamed pass at the head of the West Matakitaki Valley. Even in the warmest months of summer, crossing the river leaves you with feet chilled to the bone. A rough, permolated track leads up the true right to a series of river flats further up. Patches of prickly shield fern (*Polystichum vestitum*) and speargrass (*Aciphylla sp.*) grow on the river flats, and there are a few leg-swallowing holes amongst the tussock to watch out for. As the valley inclines, increasing amounts of rapier-leaved speargrass are encountered which require some tactical side-stepping.

The long climb up tussock slopes leads to three tarns at the valley head, perfectly aligned as if to pinpoint the location of the pass (sometimes known as the '6,000 ft' pass because of its height but not named on the map) which crosses to a creek flowing down into the Maruia River catchment. This is the sort of country that chamois love to bound about in. Introduced from Europe, chamois, along with deer, are responsible for devastating many native New Zealand alpine plants. Having evolved alongside herbivores the size of grasshoppers, the alpine plants here were unprepared for the impacts of large browsing mammals. But in spite of their destructiveness, I can't help admiring the ease and grace with which chamois move on steep mountain ledges.

Once over the pass and down to the treeline, there follows a deceptively short bush-bash to the main valley. By the time the tangle of beech saplings and ribbonwood (*Hoheria lyallii*) ends and the easy St James Walkway begins, you've just about had enough for the day. Fortunately, Ada Pass Hut is just five minutes along the

Blue Lake (SB).

well-formed track.

Ada Pass, on the St James Walkway, is an imperceptible rise between valleys which hardly deserves the name 'pass'. The popular walkway is generally easy tramping, with coal-stocked huts and good benched tracks. An hour south of Ada Pass Hut, down the

Maruia River near Cannibal Gorge (SB).

Maruia River, is the larger, more imposing structure of Cannibal Gorge Hut. Cannibal Gorge or 'Kopi-o-Kai-Tangata' – literally 'the gorge where human flesh was eaten' – came to be named after an unlucky group of Ngati Wairangi were slaughtered and devoured by Ngai Tahu warriors in the upper Maruia River. While most of this tramp over the mountains of Nelson Lakes National Park has seen foot traffic only in modern times, this section between Ada Pass and the road end at Lewis Pass was earlier used by parties of Maori travelling between the Waiau River and the West Coast's pounamu regions.

Below the gorge a bridge spans the Maruia River and the track climbs to Lewis Pass and the road from which you have your final views back to the Spenser Mountains. A quick glance at any map of New Zealand will indicate that you've covered a discernible chunk of the country, and certainly by the route less travelled.

Shaun Barnett

NELSON LAKES TO LEWIS PASS

Nelson Lakes National Park, Lewis Pass National Reserve

Length: 79 kilometres (start from Sabine Hut, Lake Rotoroa), 96 kilometres (start from Robert Ridge).

Time required: 6–9 days.

Nearest town: St Arnaud.

Best time to walk track: October to May.

Fitness: Good fitness required.

Maps (1:50,000): N29 St Arnaud, M30 Matakitaki, M31 Lewis, M29 Murchison.

Information: Department of Conservation, Private Bag, St Arnaud. Phone: 03 521 1806. Fax: 03 521 1896.

A longish trip traversing right through the centre of Nelson Lakes National Park. The trip can be shortened by two days by using the water taxi service on Lake Rotoroa to Sabine Hut. Most of the route follows well maintained and marked tracks, with marker poles over Robert Ridge and the Waiau Pass. However, two sections of the route require good navigation skills as they traverse unmarked and unnamed passes over the Spenser Mountains (often referred to as the 'Upper D'Urville' and the '6000 ft' passes). Both can be difficult in bad weather. There is only one bridge over the Matakitaki (at the junction of the west and east branches) and it is necessary to ford this river in other sections. If the weather deteriorates after crossing Waiau Pass, it's probably wise to continue out the Waiau River until it intercepts the St James Walkway near Christopher Hut. This alternative requires some river crossings, but otherwise the route is straightforward. A small two-bunk bivvy exists at Caroline Creek, on the true right bank of the Waiau.

A Department of Conservation Annual Hut Pass covers all huts on the tramp, and camping is possible beside most of these. One camp is essential at Lake Thompson. Trampers equipped with crampons and ice axes sometimes undertake the route in winter, but this should only be attempted by those with some climbing experience and a knowledge of avalanche danger. Access is from St Arnaud, a small village south of Nelson with accommodation, petrol and a store. From St Arnaud, a shuttle is available to the Mt Robert carpark or to Lake Rotoroa, where a water taxi operates (phone 03 523 9199).

Approximate track times (north to south):

Mt Robert carpark to Angelus Hut (40 bunks): 10 kilometres 6–7 hours.

Angelus Hut to Sabine Hut (30 bunks): 7 kilometres, 3–4 hours.

Sabine Hut to Blue Lake Hut (16 bunks): 21 kilometres, 8–10 hours.

Blue Lake Hut to Lake Thompson camp: 10 kilometres, 6–7 hours.

Lake Thompson to East Matakitaki Hut (6 bunks): 13 kilometres, 6–7 hours.

East Matakitaki Hut to Bobs Hut (8 bunks): 8 kilometres, 2–3 hours.

Bobs Hut to Ada Pass Hut (12 bunks): 15 kilometres, 8–9 hours.

Ada Pass Hut to Lewis Pass: 12 kilometres, 3–4 hours.

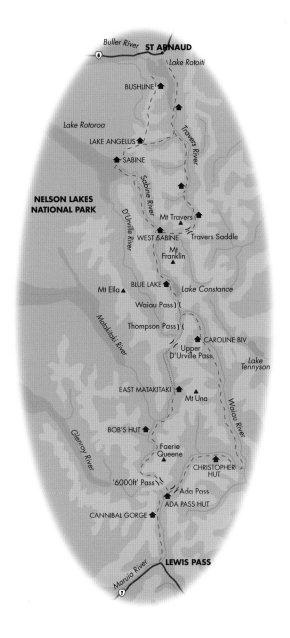

	Rivers		Over 1550 m		300–1550 m		0–300 m
	Main roads		Routes	▲	Huts	●	Rock bivvy
– – –	Walking tracks	▲	Mountains	) (	Saddles		

THE POUAKAI RANGES

In the shadow of Taranaki

Lying to the north of Taranaki, the Pouakai Range is essentially the eroded remnants of a once great volcano. Less visited than the more popular round the mountain circuit, the tracks on this range offer classic weekend tramping with unsurpassed views of Mt Taranaki (2,518 metres) and a unique perspective onto the volcanic landscape of Egmont National Park.

This tramp is a popular round trip which begins and ends at the North Egmont Visitor Centre. Right next door to the recently renovated Camphouse, one of a number of historic buildings in Egmont National Park, the tramp begins on the Veronica Walk and immediately plunges into dense, lush forest before sidling out to a thin volcanic ridge. It is one ridge of hundreds radiating from the singular point of Taranaki, and it is these landforms which will dominate the tramping in the next couple of days; for almost all of the tramp you are either slogging up them, strolling down them or (most frustratingly) sidling in and out of the ravines in between them.

Heading down the Veronica ridge to the junction with the Kokowai Track is a pleasant way to begin, and the track underfoot seems to flow naturally through the terrain. These are the sort of forest trails I enjoy walking on the most. There is nothing manufactured in the way they appear, they seem more an eternal part of the landscape than those recently hewn out by spade and saw. After an hour or so the track arrives at the Waiwhakaiho River, but a three-wire bridge over the river has now been removed and on damp days it is necessary to do a short fifteen minute detour down to a more solid swingbridge.

It was near here, on the Waiwhakaiho, that some of the early climbing history of Mt Taranaki began. Maori legend tells of Taranaki being first ascended by Tahurangi, who claimed the mountain on behalf of the local tribe. However, such ascents were uncommon and by the time the first Europeans arrived the local Maori considered the upper slopes of the mountain to be tapu. Of the early visitors to Taranaki, it was left to a young German, Ernst Dieffenbach, to throw caution to the wind and organise an expedition to climb the mountain. In December 1839 he travelled up the Waiwhakaiho River with James Herberley and several Maori companions and later wrote of the experience: "We had to walk for some distance along the rocky bed and icy waters of the Waiwhakaiho... we heeded not the difficulty as we had the gratification of seeing the mountain directly before us " – the final observation a truism which could be made of virtually any place in Taranaki on a fine day. As you emerge from the forest onto the swingbridge, there Taranaki sits, distant, aloof but always there.

At the time of his successful ascent, Dieffenbach was employed as a scientist by the New Zealand Company and was effectively living in exile because his social ideas on democracy were not popular in his native Germany. One hundred and fifty years on, the record of his journey, *Travels in New Zealand*, leaves the reader impressed

Evening light on Mt Taranaki from the Pouakai Range (SB).
Frosted Blechnum *ferns (SB).*

41

Mist isolates the spectacular volcanic dyke of Humphries Castle (RB).

with ideas which, for their time, were very enlightened. By the last chapter, as he makes an impassioned plea for equality, arguing against the accepted thinking of the times, it is easy to see why Dieffenbach was held in such high regard by local Maori.

Having descended close to 200 metres, the track now sidles along for an hour or so to Kaiauai Hut, making use of a few wooden ladders along the way to negotiate the valley walls between the ridges. Kaiauai Hut has become a little run-down in recent years, but still provides shelter from the rain for the night, that is if you can bear the rats doing aerobics in the ceiling. OK, all rats to the right of the ceiling... scamper, scamper, scamper... OK, all rats to the left of the ceiling... scamper, scamper, scamper... is usually how it goes, and so the night slowly passes.

After Kaiauai Hut, a small stream is crossed before a climb up onto a spur and the start of a 500 metre grind up to Henry Peak. The forest at this lower altitude has a very similar look to the forests on Stewart Island – tall miro (*Prumnopitys ferruginea*) and rimu podocarps and numerous rata (*Metrosideros robusta*); then a sort of middle strata beneath the taller trees where kamahi is the predominant species; and finally a forest floor dominated by crown ferns. The resemblance seems curious for two areas so geographically distant and is mainly due to the absence of beech trees. The reasons for this absence are, however, very different. Beech are thought to have been wiped off Stewart Island during the last ice age, whereas around Mt Taranaki they have been unable to close in from forests to the east because of the long history of volcanic activity. Beech is a self-seeding species (seeds not spread by carriers like birds), and it will be many millennia without volcanism before this tree creeps slowly westward to the forests of Taranaki.

As altitude is gained, the forest changes with the cooler temperatures and is mainly comprised of kamahi, Hall's totara (*Podocarpus hallii*) and kaikawaka or mountain cedar (*Libocedrus bidwillii*). As you keep plodding up it almost feels as if you are journeying into a fairy tale world where you've been unwittingly

'Goblin forest', Mt Taranaki (RB).

cast as the giant. Not only that, but every five minutes you seem to get taller! Eventually, the track becomes an alleyway amongst trees only a couple of metres high, each one laden with such delicate moss that you can't pass without running your hand across their branches to confirm that such a thing indeed exists. This band of high altitude forest, between 700 and 900 metres, has appropriately become known as 'goblin forest' and is a distinctive feature of Egmont National Park.

The rough track continues up a spur before finally reaching

Mt Taranaki from Pouakai Peak showing the erosion which continues to shape the park (RB).

the treeline and cutting its way through a thick band of leatherwood for a further 200 metres to the summit of Henry Peak. It's a good place to stop for a break and survey the 360 degree panoramic view. To the south, the Ahukawakawa Swamp (although because the word 'swamp' tends to suggest something of little interest or value, most conservationists prefer the less threatening term 'wetland') sits hemmed in by the crescent of the Pouakai Range against the northern slopes of Mt Taranaki. The view west stretches out to the ocean, which at almost any time of the day seems to shimmer with light.

Further to the east, part of the distinctive circle separating forest and farm can be seen curving around Mt Taranaki with a perfection true to the circular scribe of the map maker. A line of artifice, sure, but also a line which saved the forest from further encroachment by farming. Egmont National Park was gazetted as New Zealand's second national park in October 1900, although efforts to preserve the area had been made as early as May 1881 when it was given the status of a temporary reserve; a move which pre-dated the creation of Tongariro National Park, New Zealand's first national park, and is perhaps a testimony to the mountain's significance. The initial reserve area was a neat circle of six miles' radius from the summit of Taranaki, but two months later the Pouakai Ranges were also included.

The often muddy slither down Henry Peak is quickly negotiated, and the track flattens out to sidle around a second bump on the range, Maude Peak. On the other (northern) side of this bump, a signpost marks the junction with the Maude Track, and a boardwalk heads off in the direction of Pouakai Hut just thirty minutes away.

Eventually the boardwalk merges into an exposed patch of tephra littered with scattered lava 'bombs', and here another signpost marks the turn-off for the short descent down to Pouakai Hut. From its verandah, Pouakai Hut has an eerie night-time view down onto the city lights of New Plymouth. Depending on your point of view, or possibly just your mood, the view of the city can either

make you pine for the comforts of home or fill you with the self-satisfied feeling of being high up in a crows nest. But there is little room for such smugness during a storm when the hut shakes and shudders with every gust of wind blowing in off the Tasman Sea just 20 kilometres away.

The following day starts with a short climb back up the steps

On the track between Pouakai and Holly Hut (RB).

onto the range before following the pathway south. In the late 1800s, this section of track formed part of the standard route to climb Mt Taranaki; a more lengthy expedition than today with most parties taking a full three days to complete the round trip from New Plymouth. The route headed up onto the range from the Mangorei Road before dropping down to the Ahukawakawa Swamp and climbing the mountain from the site of the present Holly Hut. It seems an odd route to take, but in the 1860s and 70s it was possibly the most direct line from New Plymouth given the tensions of the Taranaki war.

A spur leading down from the Pouakai Range makes as direct a line as possible to Ahukawakawa Swamp and the 300 metre descent seems to take no time at all. The Ahukawakawa Swamp is a relatively new geological feature and was formed by two separate

Bells Falls thunder into Stony River (RB).

events which dammed the upper Stony River some 3,500 years ago. The first was a large welling up of lava creating a prominent cumulodome (now simply marked on the map as 'the Dome'), while the second was a large lahar which flowed down Mt Taranaki onto the south-eastern end of the dome. The montane wetland ecosystem which formed behind this dam covers some 270 hectares and is home to nearly 260 different species of plant life, including a rare divaricating shrub *Melicytus drucei*. Among the most prominent plants are flax and red tussock, while in the dampest areas extensive mats of spaghnum moss predominate. The excellent boardwalk crossing the wetland not only stops you from sinking in up to your knees but also protects the moss from being squashed into a muddy quagmire by trampers' boots.

Holly Hut is reached in just over two hours from Pouakai Hut, although undoubtedly it can be done quicker if you are happy to reduce the landscape to an unmemorable blur. However long you take, there is usually at least half the day left to explore the local environs of Holly Hut, and a good starting point is the forty minute side trip down to Bells Falls.

The falls were named after a certain Francis Dillon Bell, who organised the second ascent of Taranaki, but it would be a mistake to think that he was their discoverer. While Bell was sketching, his two companions, Carrington and a Maori chief, Minarapa, went off exploring and came across the 30 metre falls on the southern side of the Dome. On returning from the ascent, Bell, as organiser of the expedition, somewhat greedily claimed the right to name the falls after himself. Both Carrington and Minarapa were later remembered in the naming of other features near Holly Hut, but arguably the most impressive waterfall in Egmont National Park retains a name with a somewhat dubious history.

Below the falls, the Stony River area is quite different from the wetland above and is yet another distinctive ecosystem within the complex make-up of the park. The rata here have taken on a different lifestyle compared with other areas of the park. Northern rata normally begins life as an epiphyte when seeds lodge in the branches of other trees. Eventually, their roots encapsulate the host tree, which can sometimes lead to the host tree dying. But around Stony River the rata have established themselves directly on the ground and are known locally as blue rata because of the purply-blue colour of their wood.

Stony River, as the name suggests, is a swirling flow tumbling down between boulders and is an ideal environment for blue duck (*Hymenolaimus malacorhynchos*) which have recently been reintroduced into the area. Uniquely adapted for New Zealand's fast flowing mountain streams, these beautiful birds were presumed to have disappeared from the park by the 1950s. Between 1987 and 1991, the Department of Conservation released twelve birds back into the park, and the most recent survey recorded that at least half of them had established territories in the mountain's waterways.

The journey back to North Egmont is along the well-used round the mountain track and provides pleasant walking on a wide path. What seems like a staircase of a thousand steps climbs up from Holly Hut to the junction of the Kokowai Track, and from here you can look into the orange coloured headwaters of the Kokowai Stream. This area was an important source of ochre pigment for early Maori, who used it for colouring fibre and wood.

At nearly 1,300 metres, the tramp is now at its highest point as it sidles around under imposing columnar cliffs on the sides of Mt Taranaki. It is not until you are this close to the mountain that the symmetry of Taranaki, such a compelling sight from a distance, starts to be exposed for the illusion it is. Here, the important role of erosion in shaping the mountain can be clearly seen, and the scale of the gorges weathered out from the volcanic deposits is keenly felt; it takes longer than expected to progress around the cone. The same processes have eroded the Pouakai Range, once a volcano of similar height to Taranaki, and there is no shortage of water to do the work – Taranaki province is the wettest place in the North Island and North Egmont Visitor Centre receives between 650 and 750 millimetres of rain per year.

An hour before North Egmont, the spectacular volcanic dyke

Early morning light over Henry and Maude Peak (RB).

of Humphries Castle comes into view for the first time, appearing initially like the side of a large ship perched on a wave, but as the angle changes the dyke takes on a sharper profile. The sidle eventually ends where the track joins up with Razorback Ridge and a sign points downhill to North Egmont. A quick amble down the steps sees you neatly back at the tramp's starting point which, as often happens when travelling through terrain of such diversity, seems like a long time ago.

Rob Brown

THE POUAKAI RANGES

Egmont National Park

Length: 19 kilometres.
Time required: 2–3 days.
Nearest town: New Plymouth.
Best time for walking the track: All year round.
Fitness required: Moderate fitness required.
Map (1:50,000): P20 Egmont.

Holly Hut to North Egmont Visitor Centre: 6.5 kilometres, 3–4 hours.
Side trip: climb of Mt Taranaki via Northern route 7–8 hours return.

Information: Department of Conservation, North Egmont Visitor Centre, Egmont Road, Inglewood. Phone: 06 756 8710.

The Pouakai circuit is an easy two to three day tramp which can be done all year round. There is an excellent system of huts and tracks in the park, and most are well used in the weekends by local trampers. All huts within the park are covered by the Department of Conservation's Annual Hut Pass. Camping is not recommended within Egmont National Park.

The track between North Egmont and Henry Peak, via Kaiauai Hut, receives less maintenance than many other tracks in the park but is well marked and easily followed. Once past Maude Peak, the track improves considerably and the rest of the tramp is on a well-constructed path.

In summer, a climb of Mt Taranaki is safely within the capabilities of most trampers with a good standard of fitness. In winter the mountain is often icy and needs to be treated with respect. The mountain has a notorious reputation for claiming lives. An ice axe and crampons are essential in winter and should also be carried in summer. The route from North Egmont is the easiest way to ascend the peak.

Transport is available from New Plymouth to the North Egmont Visitor Centre and can be booked at the New Plymouth Information Centre, 220 Devon Street West, New Plymouth, Phone: (06) 758 0433.

Approximate track times:
North Egmont Visitor Centre to Kaiauai Hut (4 bunks): 4 kilometres, 2.5 hours.
Kaiauai Hut to Pouakai Hut (4 platforms, equal to 16-18 bunks): 4.5 kilometres, 3–4 hours.
Pouakai Hut to Holly Hut (38 bunks): 4 kilometres, 2.5–3 hours.
Side Trip to Bells Falls: 30 minutes each way.

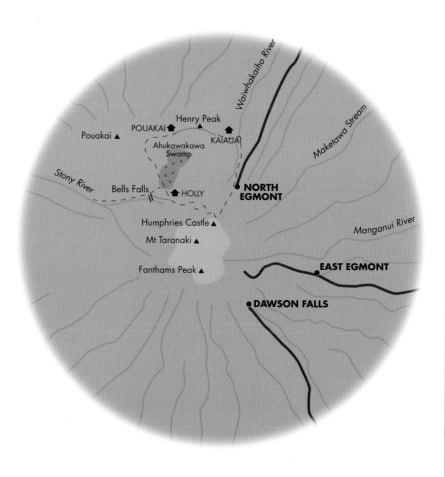

——— Rivers	Over 1550 m	300–1550 m	0–300 m
▬▬▬ Main roads	······· Routes	⬆ Huts	⬇ Rock bivvy
– – – Walking tracks	▲ Mountains	) (Saddles	

Evening light over the Kaweka Range (SB).

KAWEKA-KAIMANAWA TRAVERSE

Across the spine of the North Island

The greatest fault line in the North Island has forced up a series of mountains stretching from the Rimutaka Range near Wellington, to the Raukumara Range at East Cape. Roughly in the centre of this mountain chain, where it reaches its widest extent, are the Kaweka and Kaimanawa Ranges. A traverse across both these takes the tramper on a journey across the backbone of the North Island; from the sunburnt plains of Hawkes Bay to the pumice and ash interior of the volcanic plateau.

The tramp begins at Makahu Saddle beneath the eroded hummocks of the Kaweka Range where long ribbons of scree drain from the tops and spill into gullies. Mountain beech forest (*Nothofagus solandri cliffortioides)* grows in the wetter guts and edges over bony spurs, but for the first few hours of the tramp the topography has a certain second-hand look about it. Despite its height, the Kaweka Range attracted graziers as early as 1859, who quickly burned large areas to stimulate new growth for their merino sheep. The steep terrain and soft soils could not withstand the grazing and, combined with an explosion in the rabbit population, the resulting erosion was so severe that by 1905 the musterers had rounded up their flocks leaving only a few wild sheep. As you begin the 700 metre climb of Makahu spur, even though you know you're headed to wilderness beyond, the first impressions are, as

poet Brian Turner describes, of ranges "so badly eroded and stripped that they look like beasts in the process of sloughing old skins".

In the mid 1950s, the New Zealand Forest Service attempted to control the erosion, naturally enough, by planting trees. After trialling several different species, both native and exotic, they chose lodgepole pine (*Pinus contorta*) from the west coast of North America. An intensive programme of hand planting and, later, aerial sowing began, but despite its ability to colonise scree slopes, lodgepole pine proved to be an invasive weed which smothered native plant communities. As you climb up the poled route over shattered greywacke slopes, pockets of lodgepole pine shade the delicate eyebrights and gentians trying to grow beneath them. The Department of Conservation is systematically removing pines and aims to prevent their further spread into the park.

An hour up Makahu spur, now above the lodgepole pines, the tiny two-bunk Dominie Bivvy comes into view. A few of these stout kennels remain poked in odd corners of the Kawekas, a legacy of the deer-culling days. Bivvies served to accommodate hunters when there were not funds for full-sized huts and, where they still stand, they remain a unique part of the back country. After a lunch stop at the bivvy, a further one to two hours climb brings you onto

Dominie Bivvy (SB).

51

(Clockwise from top left) Fungus, Thaxterogaster porphyreum *(SB)*. Hebe
venustula *(SB)*. *Red beech forest and mountain cabbage trees (SB).*
Dracophyllum recurvum *(SB)*.

the crest of the Kaweka Range, from where a short poled route leads south to Mt Kaweka (often referred to by locals as Kaweka J). Here, impressive views stretch halfway across the North Island. On a clear day you can see the dry plains of Hawkes Bay and the distant blue of the Pacific Ocean to the east, while to the west lie the distinctive forms of Mt Ruapehu and Mt Ngauruhoe.

The broad greywacke crest of Kaweka J has little shape to indicate its status as the highest peak on the range, but the summit's position is marked by a memorial cairn built by the Heretaunga Tramping Club to honour members killed during World War Two. From here the route follows poles leading northward, and across the dry undulating tops it weaves its way amongst a surprising diversity of alpine plants. Growing low amongst the scanty shelter of tiny scree hummocks are rock cushion (*Phyllachne colensoi*), Maori bluebell (*Wahlenbergia pygmaea*), a buttercup (*Ranunculus insignis*) and two species of daisy (*Celmisia incana* and *Celmisia spectabilis*). Plants here have not only to survive the extremes of climate, but have also had to endure a history of human and volcano-induced fires. Along with the volcano that formed Lake Taupo, Mt Tongariro's periodic eruptions have spewed dense layers of tephra across the central North Island, destroying vast tracts of vegetation.

On parched summer days when the heat haze shimmers like a mirage, trampers must also contend with one of the problems faced by alpine plants – a lack of water. Composed of very porous material deposited from volcanic eruptions, the soils on the Kaweka Range hold little moisture, and consequently there are very few tarns. Despite drinking nearly two litres of water on this first day, the climb and scorching Hawkes Bay sun soon left me as parched as the soils.

After crossing the tops and passing the Ballard Hut turn-off, it was with some relief I descended into the welcome shade of mountain beech forest leading to Tira Lodge. During summer, the forest here resounds with the harsh calls of long-tailed cuckoos (*Eudynamis taitensis*). Arriving from various Pacific Islands during October, these devious birds lay a single egg mainly in the nests of (in the North Island) whiteheads, often pushing all the host's eggs out. Even if any of the whitehead eggs hatch, the aggressive cuckoo chick ensures the host's offspring won't survive. Oblivious to the deception, the whiteheads bring up the long-tailed cuckoo chick as their own, until the young fledgling is ready for its long journey back to the Pacific in the autumn.

After hearing cuckoos for the entire crossing of the bush ridge, you emerge onto the open tussock and scrub lands of the Venison Tops. Here, the twelve-bunk Tira Lodge occupies a small clearing on the edge of the forest. The hut is popular with hunters, who come here to stalk Sika, an introduced Japanese deer which has spread throughout the Kaweka and Kaimanawa Ranges. Sika are more wily than the larger European red deer, and thus more of a challenge for hunters. After walking all day, trampers sometimes arrive at a hut to discover all the bunks taken by hunters who have flown in by helicopter. Times like these can create tension, but as long as both groups respect hut etiquette, an evening in a crowded hut should not be unbearable. There's usually enough room to squeeze in new arrivals, and a full hut often means lively conversation about terrain, deer and equipment. One piece of gear I learned about from hunters are Bullers, a type of lace-up rubber boot, which, unlike leather boots, are cheap, light, require no care, and are just the thing for summer walking in the North Island. Furthermore, if blisters cause any problems you can simply cut the offending part of the boot out!

The Venison Tops are one of a series of knolls that poke above the uniform stands of mountain beech which dominate this part of the Kaweka Forest Park. The route from Tira Lodge leads first over a bush ridge, then across several of these knolls to Te Pukeohikarua Hut. There are a few cairns and waratahs on this section, but winter snow could make route-finding more challenging, especially in one or two places prone to drifts. A short distance before reaching Te Pukeohikarua Hut, the route passes through an area of collapsing forest, and here is bald testimony to the damaging effects of deer browsing. Whilst extensive windfalls caused by cyclones like

Beech forest near Tira Lodge, Venison Tops, Kaweka Forest Park (SB).

Bola and Bernie are natural events, the process of forest regeneration can be radically disrupted by deer. After the more palatable understorey plants like five finger and broadleaf have been browsed out, deer will target mountain beech seedlings. Sika deer, which in the Kaweka forests are more plentiful than red deer, are thought to be particularly damaging because they will browse on coarser foliage such as beech.

Deer, forest dynamics and hunting form a complex interaction in these forests, posing many unanswered questions, but without a doubt the browsing effects are so severe in areas that no replacement of canopy trees can occur. Instead, the forest is reduced to open grassland or a dense scrub of unpalatable plants. Recreational hunters rarely reduce deer densities to the necessary extent, and the Department of Conservation is currently undertaking some helicopter shooting as well as investigating other control methods. During the night spent at Te Puke Hut, if you find thoughts of forest damage as depressing as I do, a worthwhile diversion is to watch the sunset over Mt Ruapehu from the nearby tops.

The following day (the third of the tramp) brings a descent from the tops through forest to a small stream near Harkness Hut. Fifteen minutes downstream of the hut a more substantial river is reached and from here the route heads up what is known as the Harkness Valley. At first the enclosed valley forces you into the river, hemmed in by small gorges and *Dracophyllum* scrub, but later it opens expansively to red tussocklands more characteristic of the South Island. The normal pattern of stratification from forest to tussock tops has been reversed, with the entire valley floor cloaked in tall red tussock and scrub-fringed forest only on the valley sides.

The red tussock exists here and in the neighbouring Ngaruroro Valley because of burn-offs by pioneer graziers. Lower down the valley, the slow succession of tussock to scrub to forest has occurred, but at these elevations frosts have retarded the process and the tussock has persisted. Near the head of the Harkness Valley is the appropriately named Tussock Hut, situated on the bush edge. Beyond here the track ascends onto a ridge marking the western

Early morning in the headwaters of the Rangitikei River (SB).

boundary of Kaweka Forest Park.

Once across the forested ridge crest, you descend into the immense pumice terraces of the upper Ngaruroro River and cross into Kaimanawa Forest Park. There are few places in the North Island where the power of river erosion can be so plainly seen as here. In great sweeping bends, the Ngaruroro has chiselled its way down

Volcanic debris, from the nearby volcanoes, is visible on the open tops of Middle Range, Kaimanawa Forest Park (SB).

through the layers of pumice and ash soils, leaving high river terraces with undercut white cliffs. The result is a striking formation, each ledge marking the distinct downward progress of the river over time.

A descent from one of these ledges leads to the river itself. Even here in its upper reaches the Ngaruroro has considerable volume and would be difficult to ford during a flood. Once across, however, a 2 kilometre walk sees you reach Boyd Lodge, passing the airstrip *en route*. Hunters often use light aircraft to access the lodge, but with two bunk rooms and a sprawling verandah, the hut has ample space. From the deck you can enjoy extensive views of the valley and listen to the manic chatter of kakariki (*Cyanoramphus auriceps*) flitting through the nearby forest. An equally noisy, but much less pleasing companion is worth mentioning, if only because of its persistence. Blowflies can congregate in incredible densities around huts like Boyd Lodge, especially in the long-drops. Even far from such conveniences, they seem to appear from nowhere, buzzing irritatingly, just in time for your daily ablutions!

Although Boyd Lodge lies within Kaimanawa Forest Park, for the next two to three days the route traverses private land, and

permission to cross should be sought from the owners before commencing your trip. From the lodge, an at times swampy section of travel leads up the river flats of the Ngaruroro, passing through red tussock mixed with *Gleichenia dicarpa* fern and monoao (*Dracophyllum subulatum*). This is just the sort of habitat favoured by fern birds, but although you may hear their tic-tic-tic call, their secretive nature is likely to prevent a sighting. Pipits are common on the more open river flats, and there are, however, plenty of opportunities to watch them as they alight briefly, perform their distinctive tail dipping, then fly off again. Living in these open habitats makes them prone to the attention of New Zealand falcons (*Falco novaeseelandiae*), which are also reasonably common through this central part of the tramp. Patient trampers may be lucky enough to see a falcon drop from the sky with alarming speed to enfold an unwary victim in its talons.

Further up the valley you reach the junction of the Mangaamingi Stream and the north arm of the Ngaruroro River, known as Te Waiotupuritia Stream. The tussock of the north arm mingles with swampy patches and while the going is flat, mud sucking around your boots can quickly sap your energy. At the head of the valley the tussock gives way to red and silver beech forest, from where a short and gentle climb leads to Waiotupuritia Saddle. Between this saddle and Cascade Hut you are once again in Kaimanawa Forest Park, and the 4 kilometre section of forested track is a delight. A leaf-cushioned path leads amongst some stately beeches and a faint aroma like oak-aged wine wafts from the large decaying logs of fallen trees. Near a junction with a track leading into the Kaipo River, the Cascade Stream enters a narrow sculptured gorge. Further down the stream widens and the track follows along the true right bank to Cascade Hut on the Tauranga Taupo River. Being recently upgraded, the hut is no longer as damp and cold as its predecessor, but even so it's often preferable to camp beside the nearby river.

We opted to do just this, and once the tent was up it didn't take long to be enticed by the river, which we discovered had a

Sunset over Mt Ruapehu in the central North Island, from Kaweka Forest Park (SB).

Descending from Junction Top, Mt Ruapehu in the distance (SB).

good swimming hole. Summer tramping has a delightfully lazy feel about it, with long hours of daylight and plenty of time for such distractions as swimming. After a refreshing dip, it's worth a short amble down river to look at Stanfields Whare which, constructed of beech logs, a pumice chimney and sack bunks, forms one of the original huts in the park.

By now, on the fifth or sixth day, you've reached a sort of rhythm with your tramping; packs are lighter, your stride is surer, and fitness is better. On these longer trips you can almost forget the schedules of the city. Life in the hills revolves around a relaxed routine of walking, eating and, after reaching your destination, planning the route for the following day.

Leaving the Tauranga Taupo River the following morning, the route to Ngapuketurua again crosses private land. A long slow ascent ensues up a forested spur, climbing gradually to a series of knolls. At first the scrub brushes above your gaiters, but further up the vegetation becomes more stunted and rock cairns mark the way. On top of Ngapuketurua the vegetation is sparser and there are corrugations of bare greywacke gravels and soft soils which sink under your boots. Beyond Ngapuketurua's long summit, the route enters forest again, then after 3 kilometres reaches Ignimbrite Sad-

dle where the ascent to Junction Top begins. Junction Top forms the northernmost peak of the Middle Range, dividing the Rangitikei catchment from the Waipakihi River. Mt Ruapehu and Mt Ngauruhoe look much closer from here, and on a good day Lake Taupo glistens to the north. In mist, however, Junction Top is no place to lose your bearings, as there is a confusing network of spurs and a number of possible routes. Under adverse weather it pays to use a compass to navigate beyond the signpost indicating the way to Waipakihi Hut.

The twelve-bunk Waipakihi Hut lies at the head of the Waipakihi River, and from here there are several options for finishing the journey. The most direct is the poled route over the Umukarikari Range. The tops here are gentle and rolling, eventually easing to a forested descent where groups of noisy whiteheads (*Mohoua albicilla*) flock in the canopy above the well-used track. After having traversed almost 90 kilometres of great tramping country, you abruptly reach the road. No matter how tired or hungry you are, the end of such a journey is always tinged with the disappointment of leaving behind the rhythm of life in the hills.

Shaun Barnett

KAWEKA–KAIMANAWA TRAVERSE
Kaweka and Kaimanawa Forest Parks

Length: 86 kilometres.
Time required: 7–8 days.
Nearest towns: Napier and Turangi.
Best time to walk track: October to May, but avoid the roar (2 weeks either side of Easter) when the area is crowded with deerhunters.
Fitness: Good fitness required.
Maps 1:50,000: U20 Kaweka, U19 Kaimanawa, T19 Tongariro.

A classic North Island back country traverse from the parched Hawkes Bay plains to the volcanic plateau. Trampers cross a diverse mixture of terrain including shattered greywacke ranges, beech-clad ridges and the tussock valleys of the Harkness and Ngaruroro Rivers. The route crosses numerous tops, including the highest peak of Kaweka Forest Park – Kaweka J (1,724 metres).

There are ample huts (all covered by a Department of Conservation Annual Hut Pass), but a tent or fly sheet may be necessary in the Kaimanawa section between Boyd Lodge and Waipakihi Hut. The route across this section (as marked on older maps) was traditionally up the Mangamingi Stream to the Mangamaire River, then crossed the Island Range before dropping to the Rangi-tikei River and the ascent to Junction Top. But this stretch crosses private land, and the lessee of the block would now prefer the route not to be used. Instead, they recommend trampers take the route from Boyd Lodge to Cascade Hut, and then

traverse over Ngapuketurua to Junction Top. Contact Air Charter Taupo for permission (phone 07 378 5467) to cross. It will be helpful to mention you are tramping, not hunting.

A winter traverse is also a possibility for well-equipped trampers, although a large party is advisable so that the effort of travelling through possibly heavy snow can be shared.

There is no public transport to the Kaweka road end at Makahu Saddle, and buses on State Highway 1 only get within 5 kilometres of the Kaimanawa road end. The best option is probably to get a friend to drop you off at the eastern Kaweka start and walk out to State Highway 1 from the western Kaimanawa end.

Approximate track times (east to west):
Makahu Saddle to Ballard Hut (4 bunks): 8 kilometres, 5–6 hours.
Ballard Hut to Te Pukeohikarua Hut (6 bunks): 14 kilometres, 6–8 hours.
Te Pukeohikarua Hut to Tussock Hut (6 bunks): 9 kilometres, 5 hours.
Tussock Hut to Boyd Lodge (16 bunks): 7 kilometres, 2–3 hours.
Boyd Lodge to Cascade Hut (6 bunks): 16 kilometres, 6–8 hours.
Cascade Hut across Ngapuketurua to Waipakihi Hut (12 bunks): 20 kilometres, 8–10 hours.
Waipakihi Hut to Kaimanawa Road: 12 kilometres, 5–6 hours.

Information: Puketitiri Field Centre, RD 4, Napier. Phone: 06 839 8814. Fax: 06 839 8825.
Department of Conservation, Private Bag, Turangi. Phone: 07 386 8607.

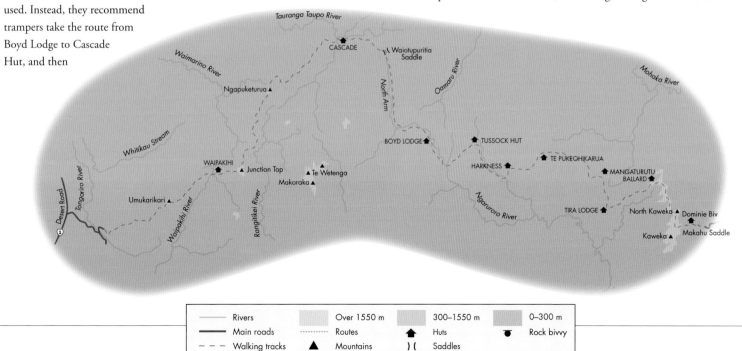

—— Rivers		▨ Over 1550 m	▨ 300–1550 m	▨ 0–300 m	
—— Main roads		⋯⋯ Routes	▲ Huts	⬣ Rock bivvy	
– – Walking tracks	▲ Mountains	) (Saddles			

CASCADE SADDLE

Soaring peaks and shrinking glaciers

During the last ice age, nearly 18,000 years ago, Mount Aspiring National Park was almost entirely submerged beneath a sea of ice. The imprints from this period of intense glaciation are today some of the icons of the South Island landscape; large terminal lakes on the eastern side of the alps, deep valleys carved into solid rock, soaring peaks unlocking the sky. Two of the larger lakes left behind by the retreating ice are Lake Wakatipu and Lake Wanaka, and the tramp over Cascade Saddle is a journey between their headwaters traversing the remnants of this ancient glaciation.

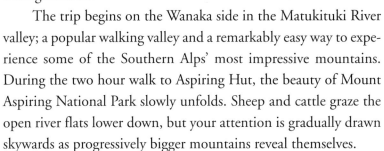

The trip begins on the Wanaka side in the Matukituki River valley; a popular walking valley and a remarkably easy way to experience some of the Southern Alps' most impressive mountains. During the two hour walk to Aspiring Hut, the beauty of Mount Aspiring National Park slowly unfolds. Sheep and cattle graze the open river flats lower down, but your attention is gradually drawn skywards as progressively bigger mountains reveal themselves.

Arriving at Aspiring Hut often has a sociable feel about it, the hut being a common meeting place for trampers and climbers as well as those who simply want to walk up for a picnic lunch. The historic stone-clad structure is beautifully maintained and the hut is fully serviced, including a telescope (used mainly for spotting the progress of climbers on Mt Aspiring) and a small supply of reading material for those wet weather pit days. Increased usage in the last ten years has meant the addition of flush toilets – sacrilege to those

who like the 'rustic' nature of long drops, but at least this new luxury has been faithfully clad in river stone to blend in with the existing architecture. Built over a number of years by volunteers from the Otago section of the New Zealand Alpine Club (NZAC), Aspiring Hut was opened during the Easter holidays of 1949. By Christmas it had become the temporary base for a group from the National Film Unit, who had turned up *en masse* to film an ascent of Mt Aspiring. The group was led by celebrated photographer Brian Brake and included a young, twenty-four-year-old poet – James K Baxter.

The film was never finished, largely as a result of the stormy weather, but the experience made a lasting impression on Baxter and became the source of inspiration for one of his most well-known poems. *Poem in the Matukituki Valley* begins with a reflection on the simple pleasures of the area from a perspective of one half-aware. As the poem progresses, Baxter's reactions become more deeply layered until, at the end, awareness arrives in the form of the landscape posing questions the writer would rather avoid.

> "Sky's purity; the altar cloth of snow
> On deathly summits laid; or avalanche
> That shakes the rough moraine with giant laughter;
> Snowplume and whirlwind – what are these
> But his flawed mirror who gave the mountain strength
> And dwells in holy calm, undying freshness?"

(Left) Mt Aspiring (Tititea) from Cascade Saddle (RB).
(Above) Rock cairn near the Dart Glacier (RB).

Frozen tarn, Cascade Saddle (SB).

While the mountains are seen to mirror God's greatness, the final verse warns how the mirror can also be turned to reveal humankind's great failure – city life and the deathly insulation that accompanies it. The final paragraph is partly mocking of those too completely taken with the urban environment, yet also confesses how most people are now only visitors to the eternal world and, after a couple of weeks at the most, once again turn their backs on wildness for the supposed safe mediocrity – the gentle dark – of civilisation.

"Therefore we turn, hiding our own souls' dullness
From that too blinding glass: turn to the gentle
Dark of the human daydream, child and wife,
Patience of stone and soil, the lawful city
Where man may live, and no wild trespass
Of what's eternal shake his grave of time."

From Aspiring Hut, it's a long two hour trudge up through beech forest to a campsite just inside the bushline below Cascade

Saddle. Unfortunately, there is only space for two tents and it's twenty minutes back down the track to water. It is, however, a useful site for breaking the climb into two and avoiding the crowds which can sometimes congregate back at Aspiring Hut.

Fifty metres further on the forest ends abruptly and the route follows the general line of a spur, with brightly coloured waratahs marking a cunning line through the steeper sections. For nearly 600 metres the trail ascends through a textbook progression of alpine tussocklands. From a distance tussocklands can be something of an optical illusion; that is to say they sometimes all look the same! But there are in fact many species of tussock on mainland New Zealand, and Mount Aspiring National Park contains some of the most impressive and distinctive examples of these alpine ecosystems.

For the first few hundred metres after leaving the treeline the environment is dominated by taller tussocks (sometimes reaching up to one and a half metres in height), the most common being the narrow leaved tussock (*Chionochloa rigida*) and the mid-ribbed tussock (*Chionochloa pallens*). At this altitude, in early December, there are often delicate Mount Cook buttercups (*Ranunculus lyallii*) growing amongst the tussock, and in places tramping can become something of a waist high wade through vegetation.

As the track ventures higher, shorter snow tussocks take over, and the curly ends of *Chionochloa crassiuscula* provide essential handholds for negotiating the steeper ground. It is a common occurrence in this terrain to ascend or descend a tricky section only to look back with a quiet shudder, imagining what the going would be like without these hardy plants to hold onto.

Just before the 1,800 metre ridge crest, the track heads out to the left (true right) onto easier ground before crossing back to the right again onto one form of tussock trampers hold mixed feelings towards. On flat terrain carpet grass (*Chionochloa oreophila*) is a pleasure to walk on, but on steep ground its short, slippery nature can be something of a death trap. In the wet, only the foolish would venture onto this sort of ground unprepared; in desperate condi-

Dart Glacier (SB).

tions even the confident will strap on crampons for extra traction. The wise wait until the rain stops and dry conditions prevail.

After a short, steep scramble up a vague, carpet grass gully, we finally emerged dripping with sweat at the old pylon point erected in the 1950s to guide trampers to this spot. The views from here are sensational. I had recently reread Douglas Adam's book *Last Chance to See*, where he described a vista in Fiordland as "the sort

A mosaic of moss colonises an old moraine left by the retreating Dart Glacier (RB).

ing back to a common point. From the saddle, the visible ice field is the Bonar Glacier. On the other side of the mountain the mighty névé of the Therma and Volta complete the sculpting trio.

Idly sitting on this ridge-top perch in the morning sun, I found myself wondering what sort of emotions the Welsh climber Bernard Head must have experienced when he reached this point as part of the first recorded climb up to Cascade Saddle in 1911. (He named the saddle after the large waterfall which cascades from it in two giant leaps into the Matukituki Valley.) Head, along with his New Zealand guides Alec Graham and Jack Clarke, had made the first ascent of Mt Aspiring two years earlier on 23 November 1909. Tragically, like thousands of others, he was not to survive the horrors of Gallipoli. It would be hard to imagine two more different experiences for a person to go through in such a short space of time, and this sad thought tempered my own initial joy at reaching the high point of the track.

From the pylon, the route sidles down a couple of hundred metres into a creek draining the slopes of Mt Tyndall, and then up a slight incline to an extensive tussock shelf, which leads around to the low point and the saddle proper. The abundance of water here provides an ideal habitat for the large white-flowered buttercup (*Ranunculus buchananii*) and stream-side profusions of marsh marigold (*Caltha obtusa*), both flowering in December. Later in summer, extensive clusters of snow marguerites (*Dolichoglottis scorzoneroides*) put on a showy display, making a friendly foreground to the backdrop of peaks and glaciers. The smell in these alpine gardens is usually the result of a number of species of *Anisotome* (members of the carrot family) which have a sweet, herbaceous fragrance.

Descending around to the low point of Cascade Saddle, the Dart Glacier comes into full view. In the last fifty years, like many glaciers in the Southern Alps, the Dart has retreated at an alarming pace, the current rate being around 50 metres a year. Glacial recession is one of the many indicators that climate change, in the shape of global warming, is upon us. There is still much debate about the cause of the steady rise in mean annual temperature, but scientific

which makes you want to break into a round of spontaneous applause". Cascade Saddle provides such a vista, due in no small part to the way Mt Aspiring (3,027 metres) anchors the eye; richly deserving its Maori name Tititea – 'the glistening peak'. I sat catching my breath and looking at the view, the composition of which had me lost for words, before breaking into a round of spontaneous applause.

A perfect example of a glacial horn, Mt Aspiring's distinctive symmetry has been carved out by the action of three glaciers work-

A small streamway provides life for a diversity of alpine plants on Cascade Saddle (RB).

New Zealand falcon Falco novaeseelandiae *(RB).*

studies seem to support the arguments citing the industrial revolution and the accompanying increase in burning carbon products as the major factors. Somewhere between 1935 and the 1960s the retreat of glaciers in the temperate zones of both hemispheres rapidly accelerated. And here is the sobering reality: humans have already pumped enough carbon dioxide into the atmosphere to keep the globe at its new, warmer temperature for the next 400 years. In other words, even if we all stopped driving cars tomorrow it would be like a band-aid on a gushing artery. As a smaller glacier, the outlook for the Dart is not good, and if the current rate of recession continues it will be gone in another eighty to one hundred years.

If you think this is being a little alarmist, or that glacial recession doesn't affect us in any way, take a seat in the tussock and look out on to the Dart Glacier. All that frozen ice you see before you is a small part of the complex energy balance which keeps the South Island working. Glaciers store energy in the winter and release it in the summer. Global warming means much more energy will be lost each winter as warmer rains corrode the glaciers instead of preserving them. In time, the balance will be changed to such a degree that the hydro lakes and farm irrigations further down will have too much water when they don't need it and not enough when they do. Obviously, this is putting it simply, but it is very naive to think that altering the climate and the energy cycles of the glaciers will not affect our daily lives in far-reaching ways.

The descent from the saddle into the Dart Valley is straightforward and begins by traversing along a tussock shelf between two vast sloping plates of rock: one dropping down at thirty degrees into the Dart Glacier, and one above which stretches up at the same angle for a few hundred metres onto the Mt Anstead ridge. The current terminus of the Dart Glacier is quickly reached and here the landscape is both desolate and dynamic. The Dart River gushes forth from the snout of the glacier, weaving its way amongst kettle tarns and recently deposited glacial till before curving away down valley. The impression is of a bleak landscape in a constant state of change.

The trail from the terminus is well marked with an assortment of rock cairns. On the descent from Cascade Saddle these cairns have become something of a sculptural art form with passing trampers making impressive attempts to imitate the work of New Zealand sculptor Chris Booth. On this part of the track they seem to appear less out of necessity, for the track is fairly obvious in most places, but more from a cheery desire to celebrate that the end of a long day is near.

By the time the track reaches the point where the glacier terminated in the 1850s, nearly 5 kilometres from its present terminus, the landscape has a more permanent feel and the old moraine flats underfoot are covered by a mosaic of mosses and small shrubs. Dart Hut is located just inside the forest across the Snowy Creek swingbridge at an altitude of 900 metres. The treeline here is 100-200 metres lower than many parts of Mount Aspiring National Park, largely due to the colder air draining down from the Dart Glacier.

(Right) Forest interior near Dart Hut (RB).

Snowy Creek (SB).

From Dart Hut there are two options for finishing the journey. The easiest is to simply continue on down the Dart Valley to Daleys Hut and then on to the Paradise road end. The Dart Valley has superb beech forests, which support an encouraging amount of native birdlife: there is a good chance you'll see the rare yellowhead (or mohua, *Mohoua ochrocephala*), flocks of tiny riflemen, kakariki and the South Island robin. But if you still hanker for the tops and the weather is good, a more interesting route is to head up Snowy Creek to Rees Saddle and then down the Rees Valley to the Muddy Creek road end.

The climb to Rees Saddle begins by first recrossing the swingbridge and then climbing up through low scrub beside Snowy Creek. About half way to the saddle the climb flattens out and a second swingbridge (which is removed each winter) crosses back to the true left of the creek. It is about here that you briefly leave Mount Aspiring National Park. For reasons that can only be clear to map makers and bureaucrats, Rees Saddle was omitted from the national park. The climb onto the saddle is completed after an hour long traverse high above a spectacular gorge which Snowy Creek has cut out of the bedrock. At 1,447 metres, Rees Saddle is slightly lower than Cascade Saddle, but still provides spectacular

views down into the Rees Valley and north-east on to Headlong Peak.

From here, the remainder of the tramp is all downhill and a poled track leads off under a set of cliffs before flattening out into an easy stroll down a basin. Just below the saddle keep a look out for mountain weta. There are a number of species which live in the alpine regions of the Southern Alps, and the population here has pronounced stripes and reddish margins – a local variation on the more common larger type of alpine weta (*Deinacrida connectens*).

Just as the vegetation changes to a mixture of tussock and subalpine shrubs, the track sidles out high above the headwaters of the Rees and slowly bends around a corner until, forty minutes before the hut, the east peak of Mt Earnslaw appears for the first time. A giant of a mountain, Earnslaw was one of the first major peaks scaled in the Southern Alps when Harry Birley climbed it solo in 1890. Although not technically difficult, Mt Earnslaw dominates the western end of Lake Wakatipu and continues to attract climbers.

Shelter Rock Hut, which is composed of one recently renovated hut and a second newer building with two bunkrooms, is located in an idyllic spot just before the treeline. It is a peaceful place and ideally suited to sleep the sleep of the dead. Tomorrow, the six hour walk through valley forests and along grassy flats to the road end will seem a long way from the stark landscape of the Dart Glacier, but take a longer look; the signs of a once mighty glacier are still present.

Rob Brown

CASCADE SADDLE
Mount Aspiring National Park

Length: 50 kilometres.
Time required: 4–5 days.
Nearest towns: Wanaka and Glenorchy.
Best time to walk the track: Late November to April.
Fitness: Good fitness required.
Maps (1:50,000): E39 Aspiring, E40 Earnslaw.

The journey over Cascade Saddle is normally started from the Lake Wanaka (Matukituki Valley) side for the simple reason it is the quickest way onto the tops. The route is well marked with cairns and poles but still requires moderate route finding ability. There are a number of excellent places to camp if the weather is fine and a well maintained network of huts.

Aspiring Hut is run by the Department of Conservation for the New Zealand Alpine Club and is separate from the Annual Hut Pass system. Currently the hut fee is $16 per night, and there is an $8 fee for camping near the hut site. A warden is present between November and April, and fees are either paid to the warden or the local Department of Conservation field centre. All other huts are operated under the Annual Hut Pass system, but it is advisable to carry a tent in summer as Dart Hut and Shelter Rock Hut are often busy.

Above the bushline, the route from Aspiring Hut to Cascade Saddle is steep and should be avoided in wet or windy conditions and especially if it has recently snowed. There have been fatalities here. Early in the season, crampons and ice axe may be necessary for a short section of snow before the pylon. The Matukituki side of Cascade Saddle is avalanche-prone and not recommended in winter or early spring. When descending to Dart Hut, the initial traverse from the ridge to Dart Glacier is above 1,500 metres and exposed to the weather. There are two flood-prone creeks between the Dart Glacier and Dart Hut – this section is not an all-weather route.

A shuttle service operates between Wanaka and the start of the tramp in the Matukituki Valley. At the Glenorchy end, a transport service operates to the Muddy Creek road end, and on the Dart River a jet boat service can be organised to pick trampers up from Sandy Flat. Check with local operators for the pick-up times as you may need to book in advance.

Approximate track times (walking from Wanaka to Glenorchy):
Raspberry Flat carpark to Aspiring Hut (26 bunks): 9 kilometres, 2 hours.
Aspiring Hut to Pylon (1,800 metres): 5 kilometres, 4–5 hours.

Pylon to Cascade Saddle (1,510 metres): 2 kilometres, 1.5–2.5 hours.
Cascade Saddle to Dart Hut (20 bunks): 9 kilometres, 4–5 hours.
Dart Hut to Shelter Rock Hut (20 bunks): 9 kilometres, 5–6 hours.
Shelter Rock Hut to Muddy Creek carpark: 16 kilometres, 6–7 hours.

Information: Department of Conservation, Ardmore Street, PO Box 93, Wanaka. Phone: 03 443 7660. Fax: 03 443 8777, or cnr Mull and Oban Streets, PO Box 2, Glenorchy. Phone: 03 442 9937. Fax: 03 442 9938.

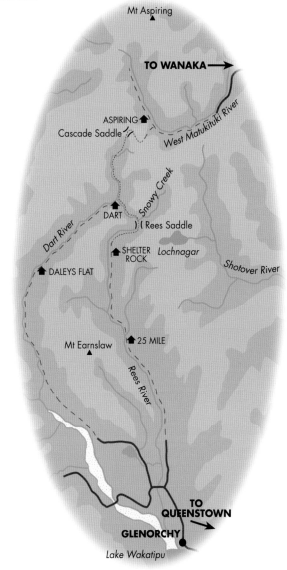

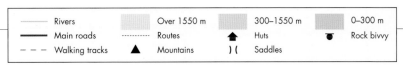

— Rivers		Over 1550 m		300–1550 m	0–300 m
— Main roads	······· Routes		⬆ Huts		⬮ Rock bivvy
– – – Walking tracks	▲ Mountains		)(Saddles		

69

THE DRAGONS TEETH

Shaped from ancient stone

When Kahurangi became New Zealand's thirteenth national park in 1995, it marked not only a recognition of the area's immense geological and biological diversity, but also a shift in attitude about what a national park should be. Before the 1980s, national parks in New Zealand tended to celebrate scenic grandeur, which meant areas like Kahurangi, with its more subdued mountains and subtler beauty, were not considered worthy of national park status. But with increased understanding about biological diversity and the importance of preserving large, uninterrupted areas containing a variety of ecosystems, the value of Kahurangi has at last been recognised.

It would be a mistake, however, to think of the park purely as a biological wonderland lacking in spectacular mountains. At 450,000 hectares, Kahurangi's immense size hides some striking landscapes from those who go only as far as the park's road ends. Trampers with ambitions for tops and challenges need look no further than a traverse of the Douglas Range on the eastern edge of the Tasman Wilderness Area. Linking the Cobb and Aorere Valleys, this is a classic traverse involving a dramatic sidle in its middle section around the high lurching spires of the Dragons Teeth. It's a route that combines hard tramping through remote country with the rewards of idyllic alpine lakes, lush herbfields and unusual granite landscapes. More than other tramps in this book, the Douglas Range requires self-reliance and navigation skills, particularly in its untracked central section where the route is sporadic.

In rocks near the beginning of the route in the Cobb Valley, 530 million-year-old fossils of a small slater-like marine creature called a trilobite have been found. They are the oldest fossils yet discovered in New Zealand (their encasing rocks are some of the country's most ancient), and their presence makes an appropriate start to a journey through an area renowned for its diverse geology.

Understanding this geology is akin to piecing together an ancient manuscript when the pages have been lost and damaged, or are barely recognisable from stains and aging. From what has been learned so far it's known that the Cobb Valley trilobites existed in Cambrian times when New Zealand was forming from sediments eroded off the Gondwana supercontinent. During the intervening hundreds of millions of years, an at times turbulent history of volcanic activity, mountain building, glaciation and erosion resulted in the present day complex hotchpotch of rocks and landforms of very different ages. The geological diversity in Kahurangi has enabled geologists to surmise much about the country's origins.

It's quite likely that as you wander up the Cobb you'll be contemplating far less colossal time scales, such as when the next cup of tea might be. Fenella Hut, a gentle four to five hour walk through tussock grasslands and enclaves of beech, makes an ideal place for a hot beverage. Perched on a glaciated knoll below Xenicus Peak, Fenella Hut combines simple functionality with charming features

(Left) The Dragons Teeth and Adelaide Tarn (RB).
(Above) Frolicking juvenile keas Nestor notabilis *(RB).*

Autumn snowfall, Cobb Valley (RB).

like carved wooden stools, a sun-welcoming verandah and a coloured window in the loo. Few huts have as much character and Fenella Hut's personal touches are due to its dual function as a trampers' haven and memorial to Fenella Druce (who with three companions was tragically killed when a hut near Mt Cook was blown away in a storm). It is still cared for by Druce family members and the Wellington Botanical Society.

Not far from Fenella, the route onto the Douglas Range starts up a swampy tussock slope and follows occasional poles to a ridge below Waingaro Peak where your effort is rewarded with views of the Cobb Valley and the enormous spread of Kahurangi's mountains. Beyond Waingaro Peak, a route of sorts, marked by an intermittent collection of blazes, rock cairns and paint-tin lids, punches through tight scraps of forest. These primitive route indicators hark back to the days before the New Zealand Forest Service's use of permolat or the more recent Department of Conservation's orange

plastic markers. Paint-tin lids nailed to trees were perhaps the first official track markers used. Often painted bright orange, they were cheap, visible and the ultimate in recycling. The lids proved far better than the once common practice of blazing, which required cutting a short strip in the bark of the tree that would eventually form a prominent scar. The method is, thankfully, no longer used as it exposes the tree to infection and rot.

Following this assorted collection of markers, the route weaves in and out of forest where stout, wiry branches of surprising strength have interlocked over the track. Mountain beech has a knack of hooking around loose packstraps or bedrolls, so in a few places progress slows to rugby-scrum pace. After a 1 kilometre stretch of tight forest, the trail emerges onto the ridge that leads towards the sloping pyramid of Kakapo Peak. From here the Dragons Teeth can be seen for the first time.

Kakapo Peak is a good place to pause and admire views, but as the track passes below the summit, make sure you gaze downward too. Underfoot is an alpine garden of typical Kahurangi diversity; vegetable sheep (*Raoulia sp.*), gentians (*Gentiana sp.*) speargrass (*Aciphylla sp.*), and snow berries (*Gaultheria sp.*) all compete for their space amongst the rock. Over half of New Zealand's 2,400 native plant species have been recorded in the park, an impressive botanical list featuring a number of alpine flowers unique to Kahurangi. Ancestors of these locally endemic plants were able to survive the milder glaciation experienced by the area and are thought to have later evolved into separate species.

I gain as much pleasure from this micro world of alpine flora, with its miniature forests of dwarfed plants and petite wetlands, as I do from spectacular mountain vistas. As well as the beauty of many of the plants, I am impressed by the strategies they employ to survive. In one tiny alpine bog I watched a trapped fly struggling vainly in the sticky clutches of a sundew (*Drosera sp.*). The luckless insect would eventually be absorbed by the sundew's digestive enzymes in what is a brilliant, if murderous, solution to the problem of fixing the essential nitrogen lacking in the mineral-deficient alpine bogs. Lack of nitrogen is only one of a host of problems for alpine plants. Some have woolly leaves to help reduce the desiccating effect of the wind, while others, like vegetable sheep, pack their leaves closely together to minimise water loss.

On the long and sometimes narrow ridge towards Lonely Lake, a low mist obscured our views, but was thin enough to allow the heat of the sun to filter through. For a few hours we worked our way along in this odd mixture of clammy heat and poor visibility before we had our first glimpses of Lonely Lake. Cradled in a cirque surrounded by bluffs, it shimmered in the surreal half-light, while Lonely Lake Hut sat almost out of sight beneath a protective umbrella of trees, an outpost of humanity on the edge of the Tasman Wilderness Area. That night we heard the plaintive cries of a male great spotted kiwi (*Apteryx haastii*), the largest of the kiwi species. Its shrill calls resounded in the cliffs and clouds, and I wondered if it was looking for a mate or merely defending its territory.

Kahurangi harbours the largest remaining population of great spotted kiwi, but stoats gravely threaten their long-term survival by decimating the chicks before they can reach adulthood. Stoats are small, efficient killers and have played a major role in the decline of other birds, including kaka and kakariki, which however still survive in reasonably large populations here. The future of these

Vegetable sheep near Kakapo Peak (RB).

birds on mainland New Zealand depends on managing predators in places like Kahurangi.

One could wish for a pair of wings on the next part of the traverse, which comprises the most difficult section of the entire route. The distance around the Dragons Teeth to Adelaide Tarn looks deceptively short on the map, perhaps only 6 kilometres as the kea flies. Don't be fooled – even with close contour lines, maps often don't represent the true ruggedness of the topography and the time required to traverse it. There are actually two options to Adelaide Tarn and both have little more than occasional route markers, meaning either route can take about two days if the navigation doesn't go well. The high route traverses above the bushline along the Douglas Range and sidles to the east of Anatoki and Dragons Teeth Peaks before finally gaining the basin above Adelaide Tarn. This high traverse is best done in the north to south direction as one very steep section (now minus the wire rope, which was removed in 1994) is safer to ascend rather than descend. Even very confident parties with good route finding skills will need reasonable visibility for an attempt at this option.

The low route involves dropping from near the prominent peak called the Drunken Sailors through beech forest into the headwaters of the Anatoki River before climbing up onto the tops sur-

Lonely Lake (SB).

rounding Adelaide Tarn. This route is best if you have any concerns about exposed, steep country, or if poor visibility deters a high traverse. Sometimes the best option is to combine both routes, starting on the high route as far as Anatoki Peak, then dropping onto the low route to avoid the steepest, most difficult section on the tops.

From Lonely Lake both routes climb out of the basin to a delightful tarn and alpine wetland beneath the Drunken Sailors where the Anatoki Peak and the Dragons Teeth can be seen rearing against the sky at truly absurd angles. The steepness of these peaks so convincingly masks the land's ancient origins (once a flat sea bed raised and tilted 10 to 15 million years ago) that it is tempting to believe the Dragons Teeth have never been anything other than

defiant mountains.

Choosing (as we did) to combine the high and low routes, the camp on the spine of the Douglas Range is likely to be a highlight of the trip. Even just finding your way to a remote camp site like this brings a sense of accomplishment not experienced when simply following tracks. At our camp site the late afternoon sun cast enormous toothed shadows over our tent, while the broccoli shapes of the forest and distant thread of the Anatoki River were already in darkness below. Watching sunrise from a camp on the tops is another of tramping's great rewards: no film, photo or painting can compare to witnessing a bruised-purple dawn sky slowly becoming splintered with bright shafts of light.

After the sun had warmed our hands and faces, and the dew evaporated from the tent, we opted to drop from Anatoki Peak via a prominent spur of stunted forest leading north-eastwards into the headwaters of the Anatoki. Once at the river, the best route to Adelaide Tarn seems to follow the Anatoki headwaters, making use of the more open river bed for as far as practical, then striking north-east through forest flanks towards Pt 1435.

Adelaide Tarn lies in a spectacular basin surrounded by mountains with apt names like Trident and Needle. Trident Hut, little more than a shed, is on a small flat terrace beside the tarn. On fine days you can swim and laze in the sun, stretch limbs and – in any weather – peruse the hut book. Huts on little-travelled routes often have fascinating log books that date back years or even decades. As pieces of informal history, they are full of wry accounts from the past about weather, trampers, epics or the local fauna. Entries recording emotional highs and lows are occasionally augmented with rough bush poetry: "The weather is all rain and gales/ But Trident Hut is rather cosy/ Tin roof battered by frequent hails/ Smell of socks far from rosy/ Inside is no spacious glen/ Two bunks here for party of ten". Some entries are more matter of fact... "John arrived here from Lonely Lake. 9 hours. On to Boulder Lake".

The track to Boulder Lake begins with a climb to the pass known as the Needles Eye. From here are perhaps the best views of

Campsite near Anatoki Peak (SB).

the trip – back across the dark waters of Adelaide Tarn with the insignificant hut a mere dot against the ominous serrations of the Dragons Teeth. Once you've slipped through the Needles Eye, there is a another section of ridge towards Green Saddle. Most of this is

Mountain neinei Dracophyllum traversii *near Boulder Lake (RB).*

just below the treeline amongst twisted beech forest interspersed with flailing, leathery groves of rough-leaved tree daisy (*Olearia lacunosa*). If you walk by in summer you will brush the faint scent of their small white flowers into the surrounding air.

Boulder Lake is by far the largest of the tarns on the trip,

partly filling an extensive basin flanked by the disorderly granite of the Lead Hills to the west and the untidy heights of Colosseum Ridge to the east. Graziers drove sheep up here last century when the hunger for grazing land was so great that even remote mountain areas like this were farmed. Then in 1899, gold miners dammed the outlet to Boulder Lake, initiating something of a rivalry between themselves and the graziers. The higher lake level allowed extra water to be diverted for sluicing operations in the Quartz Range 8 kilometres away, the task of building the water races an engineering feat in itself. Unfortunately for the shepherds, the enlarged lake covered valuable grazing land.

But the miners suffered too. Their poor old brown cow (after being forced up its namesake ridge) refused to produce milk on the sparser feed. When gold mining waned, the graziers dynamited the dam and restored the lake to its original level. During the 1930s Depression, however, miners returned to rework the gold tailings and their arrival sparked the end of sheep grazing here. Sid Flowers, who then mustered Boulder Lake as part of the large Haupiri Station, discovered that some miners had taken a liking to the 'free' mutton on the hillsides. He gave up in disgust and shifted his stock to lower pastures.

At Boulder Lake comes a choice of routes to the Aorere Valley and the finish of the tramp. The most straightforward is to follow the miners' route out over Brown Cow Ridge. As the cow would testify if it could, this is a long, dry walk with little in the way of views, and a more spectacular option is to exit via the Lead Hills, a distinctive jumble of granite rocks which look as though a five-year-old giant became bored with his building blocks and piled them into mountains.

This route first requires a climb past the perfectly round bowl of Lake Clara (named after Sid's wife) and onto the hills. While traversing this blocky landscape we were overtaken by a sudden, violent storm. The rain fell so heavily that small waterfalls soon danced through the maze of granite; we danced over the boulders too, laughing at the sheer wildness and intensity of the experience.

Granite blocks of the Lead Hills and Lake Clara (SB).

As abruptly as it had begun, the rain ceased and the clouds parted like curtains to reveal a tentative sun. Having decided we'd camp, I was fossicking around for a flat tent site when, surprisingly, a giant weta emerged to dry itself on the rocks. Unique to Kahurangi, the Nelson alpine weta (*Deinacrida tibiospina*) bristles with spines and plate armour like a medieval knight. But even this protection is no match for the stoats and rats which have forced many giant weta species like this one into alpine habitats where introduced predators are fewer.

From Clarke Peak, the exposed ridge undulates past a few cairns and onto a rough, overgrown bush track to the Aorere Valley. Re-minders of the area's past – the odd abandoned miner's pick embedded in a cairn – set me trying to imagine the hardships endured by those working in such harsh and isolated environs for scant reward, and wondering what drove them to do it. Even though the sorts of rewards that they were driven to strive for were probably very different from those motivating the modern-day tramper, part of me insists that they too would have occasionally looked beyond mineral wealth to Kahurangi's true riches – its infinite variety of ancient rocks and landforms.

Shaun Barnett

Sunset on the Lead Hills; Golden Bay and Farewell Spit in the distance (RB).

THE DRAGONS TEETH
Kahurangi National Park

Length: 53 kilometres (via Lead Hills), 60 kilometres (via Brown Cow Ridge).
Time required: 6–7 days.
Nearest town: Takaka.
Best time to walk track: October to April.
Fitness: Good fitness required.
Maps (1:50,000): M26 Cobb, M25 Collingwood.

Information: Department of Conservation, PO Box 53, Takaka. Phone: 03 525 8026.
Department of Conservation, Private Bag 5, Nelson. Phone: 03 546 9335.
Fax: 03 548 2805.

A challenging trip with long sections on exposed tops, requiring good navigation skills. The Brown Cow Ridge and Cobb Valley have well marked and maintained tracks, but otherwise the rest of the trip has, at best, only intermittent markers or cairns.

The most testing section lies between Lonely Lake and Adelaide Tarn and there are two alternatives: the difficult high route and the easier low route. Very fit trampers may accomplish this section in a long day, but most parties will prefer a camp *en route*. Good visibility is essential for an attempt of the high route, and heavy rain may flood the Anatoki River even on the low route. It is possible to combine the two routes by walking the high route from the Drunken Sailors only as far as Anatoki Peak, then dropping via a north-eastern bush ridge to the low route in the Anatoki River.

A Department of Conservation Annual Hut Pass will cover Fenella Hut and Boulder Lake; Trident and Lonely Lake Huts are free of charge. A tent is essential for the middle section of the tramp and may be needed elsewhere if huts are full.

Access to the tramp's beginning in the Cobb Valley is from Upper Takaka, and the track concludes in the Aorere Valley near Bainham. As the road ends are quite far apart, shuttling requires a few hours. Alternatively, there are transport companies who will do drop offs and pick ups.

Approximate track times (south to north):
Trilobite Hut (14 bunks) **to Fenella Hut** (12 bunks): 13 kilometres, 5 hours.
Fenella Hut to Lonely Lake Hut (4 bunks): 12 kilometres, 6–8 hours.
Lonely Lake Hut to Adelaide Tarn (2 bunks): 8 kilometres, 9–11 hours.
Adelaide Tarn to Boulder Lake (8 bunks): 9 kilometres, 5–7 hours.
Boulder Lake to Aorere valley via Brown Cow Ridge: 18 kilometres, 6–8 hours.
Boulder Lake to Aorere valley via Lead Hills: 11 kilometres, 6–7 hours.

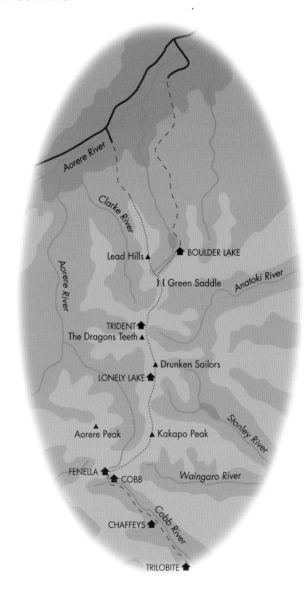

———	Rivers	▧ Over 1550 m	▨ 300–1550 m ▨ 0–300 m
———	Main roads	········· Routes	⌂ Huts
– – –	Walking tracks	▲ Mountains	) (Saddles ⏚ Rock bivvy

Carrington Peak (SB).

ARTHUR'S PASS NATIONAL PARK
THE THREE PASSES
Pounamu trail across the alps

Just an hour and a half's travel from Christchurch, Arthur's Pass is the closest National Park to any major centre of population in New Zealand. For the Christchurch tramper the park has become something of an institution – mostly as a weekend escape from the confines of the city – and is regarded with affection in much the same way as the Tararuas are by Wellingtonians or the Waitakares by Aucklanders. There are many well-known tramps in Arthur's Pass which have become perennial favourites and the Three Passes is one of the long weekend trips that seems to be on everyone's 'to do' list.

With a multitude of huts and tracks in the area, the Three Passes can be connected in a variety of ways, and a perusal of the map reveals many options for those planning their own adventure. Like many of our journeys, the trip started in precisely this way as we spread the maps on the floor and huddled around trying to come up with a plan. After much discussion, and in the best traditions of democracy (including promises which we knew could not possibly be fulfilled... "Oh sure we'll be able to do that in a day!"), we decided to start at the Styx River on the West Coast, cross over to the upper Arahura River, link the Three Passes, and then finish by heading down the Waimakariri River valley on the eastern side.

The pleasant stroll up the Styx is broken only by a new section of track which avoids a recent slip; the scale of the erosion a harsh reminder of the power of West Coast weather. In the wild areas I visit on a regular basis, I can rarely pass a changed landscape without feeling some regret. It can be a little unsettling to see the hills falling apart, and if my attachment to the place is deep enough the scars of the land seem to become scars in my mind. But of course the mountains are just doing what mountains do; they reach skywards and they fall down, and I need to continually remind myself that such events are not always isolated and human-made, but part of an on-going natural process. Perhaps there is always comfort to be had in the familiar and unchanged, but the natural world never really stays static, even if we like to imagine it does.

Grassy Flat Hut can be reached by mid-afternoon, and if you're doing the track in five days then a night can be spent here, otherwise it's another few hours' walk to the next hut. The crossing over into the upper Arahura Valley is via Styx Saddle, and, after a sticky plod through muddy tussock flats on the saddle, the route descends to a junction with the Arahura pack track.

Emerging from the rough trail of the Styx onto the old pack track brings the first hint that the journey is now entering a land with many layers of human history. Cut high into the hillside above the Arahura River in the late 1860s, the track over Browning Pass was constructed at a time when Canterbury folk were desperate to find a short cut through the alps to the burgeoning gold-fields of the West Coast. Debate raged through the Canterbury province as to the best route and work started on a second route, a dray track over Arthur's Pass, at the same time. The first flock of sheep was

Park Morpeth Hut (SB).

taken over Browning Pass and down the Arahura pack track in January 1866 and when sold in Hokitika fetched the exceptional sum of five pounds a head. But heavy winter snowfalls soon made Browning Pass more of a daring feat than a practical east-west link, and Arthur's Pass (which is 500 metres lower) became the choice for further road development.

The old pack track below Harman Hut (SB).

Today the tramper is treated to superb views through the patchy subalpine forest as the track wends its way round spurs and gullies, steadily gaining height as it makes its way to Harman Hut. Prominent in these high West Coast forests are Hall's totara, mountain neinei (*Dracophyllum traversii*) and the rough-leaved tree daisy, but noticeably absent from the forest mix are beech trees. Starting from Lake Brunner in north Westland and extending south to Lake Paringa, the West Coast's 'beech gap' is a result of the last ice age when the land was all but cleared of forest by the ice sheets that covered the area.

Ten minutes before Harman Hut, the narrow gorge of Harman River is reached. The swingbridge across this obstacle is the classic back country affair; its design having become something of a familiar icon to Kiwi trampers. It takes a bit of time to get used to crossing swingbridges of this height; their flimsiness seemingly amplified as you bounce across with just a few wire cables and a strip of wire mesh between you and the water thundering away below. But they work! It only takes a few scary unbridged crossings of rivers in flood to dissipate any fears of structural deficiencies or failure.

Harman Hut, neatly located in a cosy nook of old boulders and forest, has a commanding view of the surrounding country. From this high position, the Arahura can be seen cascading down from the pass above, collecting the flow of numerous smaller streams and rapidly gathering momentum as it heads down the valley away from the hut. Some of the boulders filling the Arahura are pounamu (greenstone), and as you head off the following day it's worth remembering that you are crossing into a river bed of special significance to South Island Maori. In a geologically young country which sometimes seems full of crumbling rock, pounamu was, and still is, prized for its hardness and beauty. Early Maori used the stone for weapons, tools and ornaments, and the Arahura is still the single most important pounamu river on the West Coast.

Traditional history records that the pass at the head of the Arahura River was first crossed by Raureka, a Ngati Wairangi

Crossing the swingbridge near Harman Hut (SB).

woman, who left the West Coast and, with her slave, made the journey east. Following a river east of the divide (somewhere near the present site of Geraldine), the pair met up with members of the dominant South Island tribe, Ngai Tahu. Raureka noticed they were shaping a canoe with a primitive basalt adze, and when she produced a pounamu adze from her kete (pack), they were quick to inquire about her journey across the mountains.

Raureka guided Ngai Tahu back across the alps to the Arahura, and a prolonged period of conflict over this highly valued pounamu source took place in the late eighteenth century. Ngai Tahu's eventual victory over the West Coast Ngati Wairangi was a gradual process of intermarriage and conquest.

In 1998, as part of the Ngai Tahu Treaty of Waitangi settlement package with the Crown, the Arahura River catchment was gazetted as the Waitaiki Reserve, with the overall management resting with Ngai Tahu, but the huts, tracks and bridges being maintained by the Department of Conservation.

Late morning on the second day of our journey and mist drifts in as we wander over the snow grass slopes leading to Lake Browning and the first of the three passes. It is early summer and on the 1,400 metre pass, winter snow is beginning to melt away leaving sculptured forms curving gracefully into exposed patches of tussock. Almost perfectly round, Lake Browning lies in an extensive basin and is easily sidled to the pass. It proves a perfect place for lunch with the mist clearing to reveal extensive views down the Wilberforce River.

Descending from the pass into the head of the Wilberforce is initially quite steep and an ice axe and crampons are useful in all

Drying socks (SB).

but the summer months. After a 200 metre descent, the route meets the old zigzag which formed the eastern side of the pack track over Browning Pass. Looking south from here to a crumbling series of ragged bluffs, you would be excused for thinking that the pack track couldn't possibly have taken early sheep drovers that way. But you'd be wrong! From the zigzags the old track cut through this

precipitous area; a route now so affected by erosion it looks a nightmarish place for stock to negotiate.

As with most of these forgotten areas, the experience of seeing first hand the efforts of those early pioneers sets our group excitedly theorising about what it must have been like in those times; a conversation which occupies the time it takes to walk downstream to Park Morpeth Hut. This recently renovated Canterbury Mountaineering Club hut provides basic accommodation and is located in a scrubby enclave at the junction of Cronin Stream and the Wilberforce River.

In the 1880s, many miners camped near the hut site while searching for their fortunes in the Wilberforce. The culmination of the efforts to find a lucrative source of gold was a series of tunnels designed to give access to what was later named Wilson's Reward Reef on the eastern slopes of Mt Harman. To say that this gold reef had difficult access is to flirt recklessly with understatement. For the Christchurch Gold-mining Company, the attempt to exploit the reef proved to be a long story of heroically blind optimism which ended in the digging of a large and expensive tunnel into the side of the mountain. Following the encouraging signs of others who had dug into the reef higher up, they dug for two years – and this is the silly part – in the *hope* that the reef ran at an angle all the way down to their tunnel. It didn't, and many small investors ended up losing money on the venture. Even after this spectacular failure, the lure of gold remained and sporadic prospecting in the area continued with the same level of success.

From Park Morpeth Hut, the journey departs the landscape dominated by the search for green and gold, and progresses over the remaining two passes to the Waimakariri River. It's a long plod over 6 kilometres to the highest of the three passes, and the 850 metre climb to Whitehorn Pass seems to have no end. The final section of snow is perhaps the most soul-destroying. Snow can play a curious optical trick in these conditions, foreshortening height, yet despite experiencing it time and again, trampers and mountaineers always seem to fall for the illusion. As we headed for

Lake Browning from Browning Pass (SB).

Snow bank beside Lake Browning (RB).

Whitehorn Pass, the snow toyed with one of our group's resolve. Her spirit dented by this cruel phenomenon, she began questioning me about other forms of ascent... like helicopters or chairlifts!

But once at Whitehorn Pass, you can relax in the knowledge that the third pass is reached by a steady – and this is the really likeable part – *downhill* shuffle through a broad open snow basin. Ariels Tarns, encircled by large red boulders and an array of alpine plants, are quickly reached and signal Harman Pass is but five minutes away. The northern side of the pass drains into the Taipoiti River, and a cairned route sidles down into this on the true left. A spectacular gorge halfway down would prove impossible after heavy rain, but in any other conditions it is a wondrous finale to a fine day's tramping.

As we leave the gorge and amble along the river flats to Carrington Hut, a familiar feeling creeps over me. It seems to put in an appearance near the end of most tramps; a quiet, reflective mood which leaves me pondering the significance of the landscape we have just journeyed through. This trip has travelled through a landscape that has, over time, felt the feet of two distinct cultures. But what is it that draws trampers today to also leave their footprints? The modern tramper has little in common with the peoples who came in search of pounamu and gold. Our contact with the land is more fleeting; we have the technology to make the journey safer; we have maps and guidebooks which erode the ability to truly discover new ground. And yet, in a funny way, trampers still come in search of riches, only they are of a non-material kind. The irony is that the new riches lie in exchanging, albeit briefly, our comparatively wealthy existence for a more simplified one; in escaping the sorts of wealth that the early explorers were striving so hard to find.

The following morning we packed our swags for the last time and prepared to head off down the Waimakariri River to the Arthur's Pass highway. The gravel bash down the 'Waimak' becomes monotonous, and I was soon once again in a reflective frame of mind, further dwelling on the question 'What is rich?'. The walk over the

Ariels Tarns and succulent early season leaves of snow marguerites (RB).

Three Passes leaves me believing more than ever in Henry Thoreau's philosophy that 'a man is rich in proportion to the number of things he can afford to let alone'. In this sense at least, New Zealand is still relatively rich.

Rob Brown

Cronin Stream, draining Whitehorn Pass (SB)

THE THREE PASSES
Waitaiki Reserve and Arthur's Pass National Park

Length: 53 kilometres.
Time required: 4–5 days.
Nearest Towns: Hokitika, Arthur's Pass.
Best time for tramping: October to May.
Fitness: Good fitness required.
Maps (1:50,000): J33 Kaniere; K33 Otira; K34 Wilberforce.

The three passes is an historic route across the Southern Alps which can be walked in either direction. The formed tracks on the western side of the divide are periodically maintained, but most of the eastern half of the trip is an unmarked route. Map reading and route finding skills are essential for this part of the trip. The passes themselves are technically straightforward and should present no difficulty to trampers with a basic level of skill with crampons and ice axe. This equipment should be carried year round as there is permanent ice on Whitehorn Pass. The main risk on this trip can be river crossings on the eastern side of the alps which are flood-prone in bad weather. These rivers generally present no problems in fine weather but quickly become impassable after heavy rain. It is not recommended you attempt this trip during a nor'west weather system. Parties caught in bad weather in the Waimakariri Valley (or sometimes if the Waimakariri is just running particularly high) can use the flood route which travels down the true right hand side of the valley via Anti Crow Hut (6 bunks). In particularly bad weather side creeks on this route can also be dangerously high and in some cases parties may have no option but to sit tight at Carrington Hut and wait for the river levels to recede.

All huts are category two or category three huts and are covered by the Department of Conservation's Annual Hut Pass. Both Carrington Hut and Park Morpeth Hut have emergency radios. There is excellent fine weather camping on Browning Pass and Harman Pass. Elsewhere, campsites are invariably a bit rough and without the compensation of panoramic views. The section of track in the Arahura River catchment (all the way to Lake Browning) is managed as a reserve by Ngai Tahu, and trampers are asked to respect the importance of this area by following the old back country adage of "take only photographs, leave only footprints".

There is a daily bus service running over Arthur's Pass which stops on request at Klondyke Corner.

Approximate track times (west to east):
Kaniere Road End to Grassy Flat Hut (6 bunks): 12 kilometres, 4–5 hours.
Grassy Flat Hut to Harman Hut (6 bunks): 6 kilometres, 3 hours.
Harman Hut to Browning Pass (1,410 metres): 5 kilometres, 3 hours.
Browning Pass to Park Morpeth Hut (6 bunks): 3 kilometres, 1.5–2 hours.
Park Morpeth Hut to Whitehorn Pass: 6 kilometres, 4–5 hours.
Whitehorn Pass to Harman Pass: 3 kilometres, 2 hours.
Harman Pass to Carrington Hut (36 bunks): 4 kilometres, 3 hours.
Carrington Hut to Klondyke Corner (State Highway 73): 14 kilometres, 4–5 hours.

Information: Department of Conservation, PO Box 29, Hokitika. Phone: 03 755 8301. Fax: 03 755 8425.
Department of Conservation, PO Box 8, Arthur's Pass. Phone: 03 318 9211. Fax: 03 318 9271.

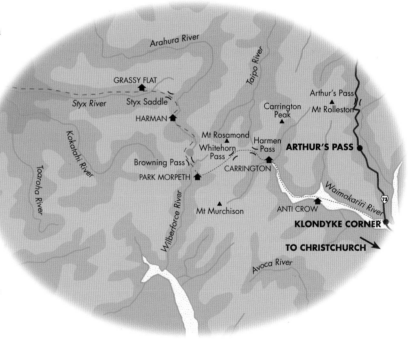

——— Rivers		Over 1550 m		300–1550 m	0–300 m
▬▬ Main roads	········ Routes	▲ Huts		● Rock bivvy	
– – – Walking tracks	▲ Mountains	) (Saddles			

Lake Roe (RB).

THE DUSKY TRACK

Into the heart of a great wilderness

Amongst trampers the Dusky Track to Dusky Sound has an attraction that goes beyond the well-groomed trails of the Milford or the Kepler. Wreathed in the earliest history of Europeans in New Zealand, Dusky Sound, with its many islands, arms and bays, combines the three great elements of Fiordland – forest, mountain, sea – in a very remote setting. The appeal of tramping through this dramatic terrain to such a distant fiord easily overcomes the area's renown for claustrophobic clouds of sandflies, mud and inevitably rain, which falls with more ferocity and volume than virtually anywhere else in New Zealand. In the words of naturalist Richard Henry, it is "fine country for the waterproof explorer", but despite the wet, the effort of tramping in Fiordland is always well rewarded.

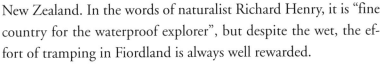

The journey to Dusky Sound begins at either Lake Hauroko or Lake Manapouri. Both routes involve a traverse of a tussock-covered mountain range and a plunge into thick rainforest before they merge, after three or four days, at Loch Maree for the final stretch down the Seaforth River to the sound itself. For practical reasons it may be best to start the tramp at Lake Hauroko because the launch service involved must be specially chartered.

Once aboard this swiftly moving launch you could be fooled into thinking the whole journey might pass at a speed that fixes a grin to your face and leaves your hair stretched horizontally behind. But any such thoughts abruptly end amongst the scattered driftwood at the far end of the lake on a shore cluttered with mist,

dense forest and thick swarms of sandflies. The start of a trip, almost always when tramping, seems more a test of endurance than something to be enjoyed. Fortunately, these sentiments are fleeting. Soon after shouldering your pack, the pleasure of moving quietly under your own energy is mixed with the excitement of seeing new country and watching the landscape unfold to reveal secrets maps never depict.

Inside the forest, an initially flat stroll along the track leads to a steady climb beside the boisterous, tea-coloured waters of the Hauroko Burn. Trampers engage all sorts of clever tricks for enduring a long, slow climb – from conversation, to blanking out all thoughts, to pitying the one who has fallen behind. My own strategy is to observe the changing forest as the rigours of altitude take hold. Tall silver beech trees *(Nothofagus menziesii)*, which at lower levels have a solid, noble shape, seem oblivious to their hefty overcoats of lichens, mosses and liverworts. Although the forest is predominantly beech, the occasional rimu emerges through the canopy.

Halfway Hut marks not only a halfway point in the climb, but also signals the start of subtle changes in the forest. Beyond, the trunks of silver beech become progressively narrower and increasingly moss-encrusted. There are occasional fuchsia trees *(Fuchsia excorticata)* shedding bark in long, red-brown strips as if someone has taken to them with a potato peeler. Consequently, epiphytes such as moss and lichen have limited chance of retaining a hold,

Evening light on the Merrie Range from Loch Maree (SB).

Lake Roe Hut in winter (RB).

leaving the fuchsia much less encumbered than the beech trees. Near the bushline the beech forest becomes stunted, twisted and gnarled from the weather's assault. Three hours from Halfway Hut you emerge from a world of green into one of golden tussock where the kaka, bellbirds, and tomtits of the forest are replaced by occasional sightings of pipits, kea and, if you're lucky, rock wrens.

A brief stroll in the tussocks on the edge of the Pleasant Range past Lake Laffy brings you to Lake Roe Hut (thankfully not called Wholeway Hut). It's worth sparing an afternoon at this point to explore the mosaic of tarns lying scattered over the intricate landscape nearby and, as it happened, convincing my companions to have an entire day off here took little effort. 'Pit days' mean the luxury of a sleep-in and avoiding your wet socks for a day, though at Lake Roe the resident keas may have different ideas about late starts. The playfulness of kea can often take on a malicious twist. I saw a tramper at Lake Roe Hut glue an ailing sole onto his boot and wedge it under the water tank overnight. By morning, the local hooligans – a bunch of feathered fiends with can-opener beaks

– had stripped all the fabric from it. When I saw him sometime later, he'd taken a pragmatic approach to the problem by purchasing a pair of steel-caps!

Lake Roe on the Pleasant Range epitomises Fiordland's magic – dark tarns amongst craggy peaks, dour mists and prickly tussocks. This is the ideal place to spend time simply wandering, contemplating and soaking in the remoteness of wild country, all without the necessity of carrying a pack.

Refreshed after a relatively mellow day, the urge to shoulder the swag and forge on to Dusky Sound returns. In fine weather the walk along the Pleasant Range is the sort of day trampers dream of, with sparkling tarns, sun-warmed for frequent dips, and a route marked by occasional waratahs amongst the tussocks. Fiordland sprawls in its immensity, with the first glimpses of Dusky Sound offering inspiration for the walk ahead. Like a distant Shangri-la it beckons with thoughts of fishing, fiords and forested reflections.

First, however, comes a gruelling geography lesson on U-shaped valleys in the form of the descent to Loch Maree. From the tops the

(Left) Fresh snow on the Pleasant Range (RB).

A three-wire bridge, one of many between Loch Maree and Supper Cove (SB).

track begins a knee-torturing, 1,000 metre plunge through near-vertical forest to the gentle valley floor. You can't help but admire the way trees eke out an existence on such steep insubstantial soils. Centuries ago a large chunk of rock and soil gave up its precarious hold on the valley wall and, like someone learning to ski on a crowded slope, crashed headlong downwards sweeping all before it. The debris dammed the sluggish Seaforth River, drowning the forest behind it and creating the small Loch Maree. In the dark moods of dawn and dusk the dead tree trunks are stark memorials to the former forest. Loch Maree Hut sits on a small peninsula jutting into the lake and is where the north and south tracks join.

The journey down the lower Seaforth Valley to Supper Cove and Dusky Sound is a comfortable overnight side trip from Loch Maree. There's little point in carrying all your food to the sound, so heave spare food into a bag and leave it for your return, making sure it's secure from mice.

Almost as soon as you leave Loch Maree for Supper Cove, the track becomes benched with the distinctive imprint of an old road,

which is exactly what it was intended to be! In 1903, Prime Minister Dick Seddon posted fifty unemployed West Coast miners to Supper Cove with instructions to build a road towards Lake Manapouri – a far-fetched proposal from politicians with minds clouded by the economic recession. The vessel *Hinemoa* delivered the men to the thick folds of the forest, then left them to the mercy of the rain and sandflies. Using hand tools they hacked a wide trail beside the Seaforth. Mercifully, the futile project was soon abandoned, though not before almost 10 kilometres of remarkable endeavour had been completed. A few discarded tools, now firmly in the grip of rust, remain at one point on the trail; small reminders of the enormous effort made to carve out a road in such demanding country.

Despite the old road, the day's walk from Loch Maree to Supper Cove is no Sunday stroll. There is mud in abundance, numerous stream crossings, and sandflies large enough to arouse suspicions of steroid abuse. Three-wire bridges span eight streams on the six hour walk, though all but three are unnecessary except when

The ghostly remains of the forest drowned by Loch Maree (SB).

Early morning light filters through beech forest, Hauroko Burn (RB).

Fiordland deluges produce bullish, flooding creeks.

The Seaforth ends its reluctant loiter down valley when it finally merges with the tidal head of Dusky Sound at Supper Cove. At low tide it is possible to work your way around the coast to Supper Cove Hut, a much more pleasant alternative to the energy-sapping sidle in forest around the steep walls of the sound. Supper Cove Hut will often be heralded by an encouraging cowlick of smoke curling into the forest. This is indeed a welcoming sight for those who may have endured, as we did, six hours of rain from Loch Maree. Once inside, a flurry of activity sees dripping garments jostling for position around the fire, and the luxury of pulling on dry clothes sends warm shivers right to the soul.

Warm, dry and fed, the urge to venture outside returns, but just beyond the hut's fly-screened armour await demented hordes of sandflies eager to probe vulnerable scalps, ears, noses and any forgotten holes in trusty old longjohns. Maori legend tells us sandflies were a curse cast over Fiordland to protect its astonishing beauty – a tactic that seems to have worked.

On my first visit to Supper Cove, we rowed a small dinghy into the fiord. The bow of the borrowed clinker corrugated the water with ripples that spread away and momentarily disrupted perfect reflections on the mahogany surface. Surrounded by forest, Dusky Sound was dark and brooding, its depth impossible to judge, and as we rowed centuries seemed to slip away. Captain Cook named the sound Dusky Bay during his first voyage to New Zealand in 1770, although unfavourable winds drove him past before he could investigate the promising harbours within. But he had not forgotten its potential, and on his return voyage with the *Resolution* and the *Adventure* in 1773, found anchorage at what is today known as Ship Cove in Preservation Inlet. Cook and his men stayed five weeks, replenishing supplies, surveying the sound and naming many of its features: Five Finger Point, Resolution Island, Luncheon and Supper Coves.

Cook left an accurate chart of Dusky Bay, which, along with reports of ample fur seals, focused future attention on this southwestern corner of New Zealand. The sealers eventually came and, in 1792, established on Anchor Island (in the outer sound) New Zealand's first European house, settlement and business venture. Fur seal pelts were in high demand for hats in the fashion houses of Europe, and by the 1820s fur seals were just a few hats away from extinction. Having brutally exploited one resource, the sealers traded cudgels for harpoons, and southern right whales became their next quarry until they too were virtually gone. Camps were abandoned and Fiordland was left alone, at least for a while. Back on our dinghy, we rowed about the fiord at the same slow, steady pace that Cook's navy cutters would have moved within a setting that has changed little since his visit. We paused to fish with small hand lines, but in the grandeur of this landscape fishing was almost a distraction.

Supper Cove, like the summit of a mountain where the uncertainty of having only half completed the journey mixes with a strong desire to linger, is a difficult place to leave. But eventually, such desires must be overcome and the way to Loch Maree retraced. Once beyond the Loch on the track to Manapouri, the Seaforth at last gains a momentum befitting a Fiordland river. The forest closes in on the track which returns to normal width, and boggy stretches require a gymnastic hopscotch approach to avoid the worst of the mud. (This section is particularly prone to floods if the weather turns nasty, which can enforce a wait at Loch Maree.)

Kintail Hut near the head of the Seaforth offers a last respite before the 800 metre climb to Centre Pass. About three-quarters of

an hour after the hut, the track ascends a 200 metre section through steep forest laced with convenient ropes and a staircase of tree roots. This is undoubtedly the most arduous section of the track, but even bursting lungs and aching thighs are preferable to the alternative of coming from the other direction and descending with a heavier pack.

On a good day, Centre Pass is another place to pause and admire the mountainous stern of New Zealand. The triangular bush knob of Tripod Hill draws attention because of its unusual shape, while the Seaforth stretches beyond and mountains shoulder over the main valley, ridge after ridge obscuring countless smaller side valleys. Here, I find myself awed by Fiordland's vastness. Only the major features have names, and within the complex folds of the

Supper Cove Hut (RB).

land are countless unknown, barely explored niches. All this wilderness induces a meditation on landscape and the immense forces that have shaped it – aeons of up-faulting, glaciation and weathering. Eventually, late afternoon breezes pull me from my contemplation, and my thoughts turn to the northerly views of the upper Spey Valley, and the route out.

Thomas Mackenzie first explored the upper Spey with two

Mist clearing from the Seaforth Valley (RB).

Blue duck Hymenolaimus malacorhynchos *(Steve Baker)*.

Wildness as far as the eye can see: the Seaforth Valley from Centre Pass (RB).

companions, Murrell and Pillans, in 1894. They discovered three passes, all leading into the head of the Seaforth River, an area Mackenzie had already partially explored. Mackenzie, however, (after Pillans had lost the compass) confused the bearings and thought he'd discovered a new valley, promptly naming it after himself. Not until 1897 was his mistake corrected by the more meticulous surveyor E.H. Wilmot. Wilmot became the first European to complete the route from Manapouri all the way to Supper Cove, though none of these explorers used Centre Pass, which was not discovered till much later.

The descent from Centre Pass into the upper Spey is, thankfully, gentler than the one down to Loch Maree. But approaching Upper Spey Hut for your last night on the Dusky Track presents mixed feelings – disappointment at the end of a journey contends with the undeniable pull of home, food and showers now only a day away. The final leg follows the Spey River to the Wilmot Pass road. It's an unlucky tramper who by this time has not spied at least one pair of blue duck on either the Hauroko, Seaforth or the Spey Rivers. As someone with less-than-basic whitewater kayaking skills, it's a pleasure to watch these superbly adapted birds. They seem to instinctively understand the current, using short bursts of speed to glide across rapids. Even the small fledgling ducks seen in summer have mastered the most turbulent cataracts, deftly weaving and bobbing around boulders.

After days spent in the heart of Fiordland, the Wilmot road and power lines come as blatant reminders of civilisation. If the tour-bus drivers returning from Doubtful Sound won't oblige you with a lift, it's a forty-five minute plod down the road to the jetty at Lake Manapouri. Settled amongst the tourists on the boat across the lake, you can feel a glow of satisfaction despite smelly clothes and an unkempt appearance. Fiordland reveals itself more fully to those willing to walk its tracks.

Shaun Barnett

THE DUSKY TRACK

Fiordland National Park

Length: 80 kilometres (including 4 kilometres from track end to Lake Manapouri along Wilmot Pass Road).
Time required: 7–9 days.
Nearest towns: Tuatapere, Manapouri.
Best time to walk track: December to March.
Fitness: Good fitness required.
Maps (1:50,000): C44 Hunter Mountains, C43 Manapouri, B44 Resolution.

The Dusky Track covers a sizable chunk of southern Fiordland and requires a higher degree of fitness than any of the Fiordland Great Walks. Although the route is well marked and all major stream crossings have three-wire bridges, sections of the track can become impassable after heavy rain. The Supper Cove to Loch Maree section is particularly flood prone. Trampers must not underestimate the seriousness of these sections; take extra food and be prepared to wait – there are some deep, back-water guts which quickly become chest-deep or uncrossable when the Seaforth River floods.

One other section which can cause difficulty is the Seaforth River crossing to Loch Maree Hut after the descent from the Pleasant Range. Currently a very long three-wire bridge spans the river, and the Department of Conservation plans to replace this with a footbridge. However, even access to the bridge may be cut off by high water levels, and a small shelter will be built for those parties having to wait out floods. Centre Pass and the Pleasant Range are both exposed to storms and, despite marker poles, may require navigation in very bad visibility. There are good huts at regular intervals and all are covered by the Annual Hut Pass. Camping is possible on both the Pleasant Range and Centre Pass.

Transport arrangements need to be planned in advance, as the Lake Hauroko launch requires booking. Launch services operate two to three times daily across Lake Manapouri in summer. For those with less time, a float plane can be chartered into Supper Cove, reducing the walk to a four-day trip back to Manapouri.

Approximate track times (south to north):
Hauroko Burn Hut (8 bunks) **to Halfway Hut** (12 bunks): 11 kilometres, 4–6 hours.
Halfway Hut to Lake Roe Hut (12 bunks): 7 kilometres, 3–4 hours.
Lake Roe Hut to Loch Maree Hut (10 bunks): 7 kilometres, 4–6 hours.
Loch Maree To Supper Cove Hut (12 bunks): 13 kilometres (one way), 6–7 hours.

Loch Maree to Kintail Hut (12 bunks): 10 kilometres, 6–8 hours.
Kintail Hut to Upper Spey Hut (10 bunks) via Centre Pass: 7 kilometres, 5–6 hours.
Upper Spey Hut to Lake Manapouri: 12 kilometres, 5–6 hours.

Information: Department of Conservation, PO Box 29, Te Anau. Phone: 03 249 7924. Fax: 03 249 8515.
Lake Hauroko Tours, No 1 RD, Tuatapere. Phone: 03 226 6681.

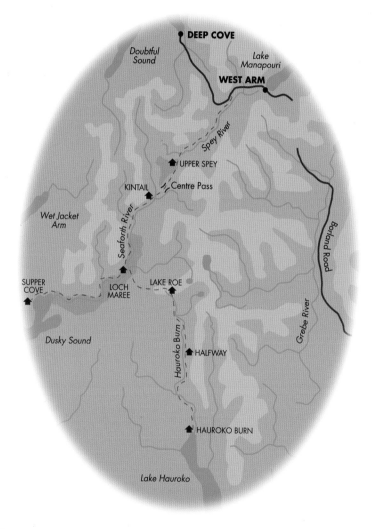

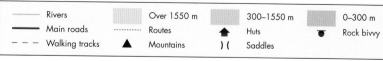

——	Rivers		Over 1550 m		300–1550 m	0–300 m
——	Main roads	··········	Routes	▲	Huts	Rock bivvy
– – –	Walking tracks	▲	Mountains	)(	Saddles	

Lake Diana (Robin Smith).

MOUNT ASPIRING NATIONAL PARK
MAKARORA TO THE EAST MATUKITUKI

Two alpine passes, four forest valleys

Lake Wanaka, New Zealand's fourth largest lake, stretches for nearly 40 kilometres along the eastern margin of Mount Aspiring National Park and is fed at its northern end by the Makarora River. Flowing into the southern end of the lake is the Matukituki, a river of similar size. The journey traversing from the Makarora up the Young and Wilkin Rivers (two of the Makarora's larger tributaries) and into the east branch of the Matukituki requires the linking of two popular smaller tramps, more often done as separate adventures.

Combining these two walks gives a ten day tramp which traverses two high alpine passes; Gillespie Pass, a crossing east of the main divide between the Young and Wilkin Rivers; and Rabbit Pass, which links the Wilkin with the East Matukituki River. The tramping in between these high points is often easy walking in forested valleys, then as height is gained the terrain turns to alpine meadows bordered by steep mountains. Throw in the advantage of starting on easier ground when packs are heavier and finishing with a couple of days travel in a more remote part of the park when packs are lighter, and you have transalpine tramping *par excellence*.

Two and a half kilometres up the road from Makarora, the journey up the Young River valley begins with a careful crossing of the Makarora River (near its junction with the Young) before entering into the forest. A good track leads along the riverbank through one of the most impressive beech forests in the South Island. Its brimming health is evident in the numerous riflemen (*Acanthisitta chloris chloris*) which appear at regular intervals along the track. The smallest of our forest birds (not much larger than your thumb) and our only surviving bush wren, riflemen are a gregarious forest bird often seen in flocks as they systematically scour tree trunks for small invertebrates.

After crossing a swingbridge spanning the north branch of the Young River, the track arrives at a designated Department of Conservation camp site with established toilet facilities, an open shelter for cooking and a fireplace. Armed with sandfly repellent it makes a tolerable place to spend the night. The camp is located near the junction of the north and south branches of the Young River, and from here the track turns into the south branch and climbs steadily up to Stag Creek. Keep a close lookout around this creek for a rare, canary-like bird – the yellowhead or mohua. Often heard before they are seen, their metallic trill is one of the most distinctive sounds in the forest, and Stag Creek is a good place to see a group noisily feeding from tree to tree. Their North Island counterparts, whitehead, have survived introduced

Often heard before they are seen, a yellowhead Mohoua ochrocephala *searches for insects in the beech forest of the Young Valley (RB).*

103

predators reasonably well, mainly because they build open nests. Yellowhead, however, nest in holes, making the females extremely vulnerable to stoat predation, and have consequently fared much worse. Sometimes it seems something of a miracle that there are any of these small birds left at all, and there probably wouldn't be were it not for a concerted effort by Department of Conservation staff to save what is left.

For the last 400 metres to the bushline, the track passes through groves of ribbonwood trees, which often grow on the fringe of sil-

Morning light strikes the northern aspect of Mt Awful, the dominating view from Gillespie Pass (RB).

ver beech forest at this altitude. In late February, when the ribbonwood is in full flower, the white petals of fallen blooms cover the most common fern in these higher forests – the prickly shield fern. Eventually, the track emerges from the forest into a tussock-filled basin. Perched at the edge of this basin with a spectacular view back down the valley is Young Hut; a well maintained ten-bunk building with a snug design and pot belly stove to pump out the heat when the weather turns cold.

Twenty minutes up the basin from Young Hut, the climb to Gillespie Pass begins underneath the imposing north face of Mt Awful and continues at a consistently steep grade for 500 metres. There is no chance for a gradual warm up as the track literally steps from the flat into the climb with no moderate ground in between. In recent years the crossing has been subject to the plodding boots of an increasing number of trampers, and a staircase of sorts has been fashioned into the ground. The track seems to be getting just about the right amount of wear. Any less and the steps would become lost in the vegetation, any more and they would soon erode.

From Gillespie Pass itself there are stunning views; the sort of panoramas usually only gained from the summit of high peaks. The pass has a few rocky areas and in late summer edelweiss (*Leucogenes grandiceps*) can often be found sheltering in cracks, withered stragglers hanging on till the last as edelweiss tends to do.

There is limited but spectacular camping on Gillespie Pass, and on the calm still evening we were there it seemed the obvious thing to do. Our tent was not up five minutes before there was a flash of scarlet feather and a kea (*Nestor notabilis*) glided by shouting out its name – 'kee-yah, kee-yah'. The comedian of the mountains was back for another show. After a few moments the friends of the young bird arrived, six of them winging their way in, expertly grappling with the gusts of wind in a masterly display of flying. The rowdy gang hopped up to see what there was to investigate. It's the sort of behaviour you either love or hate, but I'm usually won over by their demonstrations of friendly curiosity and willing to let them temporarily poke around at a few bits of gear.

Eventually, they get bored with creating wreckage and just hang around for a bit of companionship; their initial loudness being replaced by a more gentle call.

More orange waratahs lead leftwards from the pass before dropping down to Gillespie Creek where sheltered camping can be found if the weather is more inclement higher up. The river flat is quickly crossed and before long the track is back in the beech forest and descending down to the extensive flats of the Siberia Valley. Perhaps one of the most wonderful things about the beech forest in the Siberia is that there are trees here at all. By the 1930s it was recognised that introduced red deer were having the same impact on the forests as the last ice age, the main difference being that the destruction was happening much faster. To their credit, successive governments took steps to curb the problem, but despite the heroic efforts of many full-time ground shooters throughout New Zealand, numbers continued to increase in the back country. By 1961, the problem had become so bad in the Siberia that a climbing party counted one herd of 300 deer grazing the flats and shrublands.

Then something of a conservation miracle happened. In the mid 1960s, helicopters arrived on the scene and were immediately utilised as aerial gunships, giving access to even the most difficult terrain. A few years later, when the recovery of venison was at its peak, up to fifty machines were operating in Mount Aspiring National Park, combing every valley for the pests, which were, all of a sudden, the new gold of the hills.

But if the forests were saved, the open tussock flats of the Siberia were not. Contrary to appearances, tussock flats are extremely fragile plant communities and once aggressive grasses and weeds take hold in the soil there is little hope of reversing the process. As you wander amongst the waist high grass of the Siberia, it's easy to slip into thinking that the area is quite idyllic. There is no denying the valley is still beautiful, and yet because of grasses more suitable for grazing being deliberately introduced some time ago, the Siberia flats are also something of an ecological disaster. If you look

A lonely iceberg is all that remains in late summer on Lake Crucible (SB).

down between your feet you start to realise that these grasses have colonised the flats so comprehensively that virtually no native tussock remains. The most predominant sign of anything native are the pale flowers of the bluebell.

The large Siberia Hut is a popular destination for overnight trampers, who often fly in via the airstrip and walk out to the Wilkin Valley. It's worth spending an extra day here to explore the Lake Crucible area. An hour back up the flats, a track climbs steeply up through forest before flattening out onto an open basin; by now a

Approaching the Waterfall Face (RB).

familiar pattern of ascent into any glaciated valley. Lake Crucible itself is quite small and acts as a sort of reservoir for the water draining down the ramparts of Mt Alba's north-eastern face. Often seen amongst the moraine boulders which dam Lake Crucible is New Zealand's only true alpine bird. When winter snows cover the tops most other birds head down to lower levels, but the tiny rock wren (*Xenicus gilviventris*) ekes out a living in the maze of small tunnels in the rocky jumble. A poor flyer, the rock wren's behaviour is more akin to that of a mouse, scampering amongst the boulders, pausing only to perform its distinctive bowing and bobbing display.

From Siberia Hut, a straightforward three hour walk leads down to the junction of the Wilkin and Siberia Rivers. This marks the end of the first half of the journey and parties only doing the Young–Wilkin part of the tramp generally jet boat back down to Makarora from here. For those continuing to Rabbit Pass, the Wilkin River needs to be crossed. There is no bridge here and even at normal flow it takes a bit of searching to find a suitable place to ford. Once on the other side, Kerin Forks Hut is located in a clearing just a couple of minutes away and marks the start of the second half of the journey.

Kerin Forks Hut is mostly used as a lunch stop for those doing the longer journey, after which a steady plod for four hours up the banks of the Wilkin leads to Jumboland Flats. Near here, in the forests of the Wilkin, the last confirmed sighting of the South Island kokako (*Callaeas cinerea cinerea*) was made in 1958. In the late 1980s, a number of unconfirmed sightings were reported in the Young Valley, but now the survival of this ancient wattle bird seems very unlikely.

It's easy walking from the flats for a further two hours to Top Forks Hut, located near the junction of the north and south branches of the Wilkin. To the north, the mountains of Castor and Pollux soar up nearly two vertical kilometres and are an arresting sight from the hut's verandah. In the past few years this spot has become increasingly popular and to cope with the peak season pressure on the old six-bunk hut it was decided more accommodation was

needed. The park management took the decision not to pull down the old New Zealand Forest Service hut and erect a large replacement 'barn'. Instead they made the enlightened choice of building a complementary ten-bunk hut; a move which makes both huts

A winter sheet of ice covering Lake Castalia slowly breaks up with the onset of spring (RB).

cosy and easy to heat, especially at off-peak times when there are only a few trampers needing a roof over their heads.

Top Forks is a great place to stay an extra day, and venturing up to the lakes of Castalia, Lucidus and Diana is highly recommended. An hour's walk from Top Forks, Lake Diana is reached;

Huts at Top Forks under the flanks of Mt Ragan (SB).

an overgrown tarn occupying a depression in the moraine on the margin between forest and tussock. Further up valley, the second of the lakes, Lucidus, is both the largest and the most active. The icebergs floating in its chilly waters are an indication of the forces at work, but it is still something of a shock to be sitting in the sun and have the peace shattered by an avalanche crashing down into it from the ice fields of Castor and Pollux above. You tend to see these avalanches before you hear them, a white floating cloud descending like a silent assassin before the rising thunder of ice and rock in collision.

Tucked away high at the end of this valley, the final lake of the trio, Castalia, is surrounded by an amphitheatre of steep walls scooped out relatively recently by the movement of a glacier. On the spring day we were there, winter ice covering the lake had only partially melted giving the landscape an almost Antarctic-like appearance.

There is a magic in this valley which takes hold as the day wears on, and as we retraced our steps back down there was an unspoken reluctance to leave. We lingered at Lake Diana until the evening light had left the valley before scampering back down to the hut for a much needed brew.

From Top Forks Hut, the track climbs steadily up to the bushline and into yet another high alpine meadow. The key to crossing over Rabbit Pass is the ascent of the Waterfall Face. This route is not to be underestimated and could prove lethal in wet or snowy conditions. Old waratahs out to the right of the waterfall go straight up steep ground before traversing back over a set of bluffs. While it is important not to be too tentative in this kind of situation, a cautious check of every foot placement, and a gentle test of each tussock handhold is a wise precaution here.

The scary section finishes high above the stream which feeds the waterfall, and here there are more friendly tussock slopes in which to sit down and think about how good life is (and maybe offer some silent words of thanks to the mountain gods). The rest of the route to Rabbit Pass is a pleasant amble up a beautiful basin; a good chance to settle your nerves and start to appreciate the grandness of the location. Rabbit Pass itself is at the basin's head and was so named by the explorer Charlie Douglas in his belief that rabbits used the route to swarm from Otago over into the Waiototo River.

On one trip over the pass we camped the night in this alpine basin only to wake in the morning to a swirling storm of damp sleet – a typical spring tramping weather change. When the weather breaks at this altitude, doing the simplest tasks with a practised efficiency is often the difference between a safe escape and disaster. Packing up our camp was, as usual, dominated by two priorities – keeping the hands warm and ensuring nothing blew away, with breakfast reduced to a hastily devoured chocolate bar.

The descent off Rabbit Pass begins by following a poled route towards Mt Lois for around thirty minutes before a steep gully leads down through the bluffs. With visibility down to only a few metres, finding this gully was something of a relief and, still full with winter snow, it provided straightforward down climbing (crampons and ice axe essential) to safer ground.

From the gully, height is quickly lost down tussock slopes, normally a pleasant stroll, but for us the storm intensified. Gusts of wind saturated with frozen crystals were visibly building high up on mountain walls before descending in violent waves. It was like being caught in a surging ocean of air, and at one point travel became so difficult there was no option but to crawl down a wind-raked spur for 50 metres or so.

After a descent of some 500 metres, the track levels out onto the river flats of the East Matukituki, and a further hour's travel down river leads to Ruth Flat which, after the rain, had become an extensive soggy wetland. At the end of a long trying day it is a bit depressing to then have to wander around in persistent drizzle for half an hour to find a suitable place to camp. But this is often the nature of tramping in remote areas; life becomes just that little bit more testing with no cosy hut to dry out gear.

Leaving Ruth Flat, a rough track sidles up an achingly slow climb to the bushline before descending beside Hester Pinney Creek at the bottom end of Bledisloe Gorge. In fine weather the view from the bushline is an impressive vista of the steep walls of the Kitchener Cirque, but enveloped in a sou'wester it was the chance to experience a different sort of beauty. The temperature had continued to drop, and for the last couple of hours snow had begun to steadily decorate everything it touched.

Descending the spur to Kitchener Flat takes around an hour and once there it's a matter of linking arms to cross the east branch of the Matukituki River and then Kitchener Creek. There is no flood bridge across either of these rivers and in bad weather both can become impassable. Once on the other side, the maintained track through the forest erodes any edginess which may have built up over the last two days. I'm often surprised when I hear people relate their fear of the bush to me. For many trampers the forest is a safe refuge, home to nothing with malicious intent. After two days of epic weather on the tops, the forest seemed a haven; it's times like these you really do want to 'hug a tree' – to sit underneath and be thankful for its shelter as the wind roars through its limbs.

After three hours walk down the East Matukituki, the track suddenly bursts out onto open grassy flats. Strolling through open paddocks to the quizzical looks of grazing sheep and cattle is An odd way to finish ten days in the wilderness. Nonetheless it gives a good hour or so to readjust before hitching a ride down the dusty road to Wanaka.

Rob Brown

In the basin above the Waterfall Face, still covered in winter's snow (RB).

Descending to Junction Flat in a spring snow storm (RB).

MAKARORA TO THE EAST MATUKITUKI

Mount Aspiring National Park

Length: 84 kilometres.
Time required: 8–10 days.
Nearest towns: Wanaka and Makarora.
Best time for walking the track: December to April.
Fitness required: Good fitness required.
Maps (1:50,000): F38 Wilkin, F39 Matukituki.

This journey is composed of two shorter trips joined into one: the Gillespie Pass tramp (which links the Young and the Wilkin valleys) and the Rabbit Pass trip (which links the Wilkin and the East Matukituki valleys). Gillespie Pass (1,490 metres) is a pleasant, straightforward crossing with well marked and maintained tracks. Parties opting to only complete this section of the tramp can either jet boat out from the Wilkin–Siberia junction or walk out down the Wilkin River to Makarora (6–8 hours).

The second half of the tramp starts by following up the Wilkin River on a good track to Top Forks Hut. The tramp gets considerably harder from here and crossing Rabbit Pass (1,430 metres) requires ascending the steep 'waterfall face'. This requires sound backcountry experience to safely negotiate and presents an entirely different level of risk compared to Gillespie Pass. The route up the waterfall face starts on the far right hand side as you look up. Pick up the marker poles and follow these straight up before traversing back to the left above steep bluffs, exiting the face 150 metres above the head of the waterfall. This traverse is on steep snow grass slopes; a slip here would be difficult to stop and would most likely be fatal. In no circumstances should you attempt to ascend or descend this section in wet conditions.

Descending Rabbit Pass into the East Matukituki can also present some difficulty. In summer, the route heads down a rock gully for 30 metres. Some parties may want to take a short length of rope to lower packs down before scrambling down without the extra burden. The East Matukituki is very much a remote experience area with no bridges or huts. Several river crossings can become impassable in bad weather and a tent is essential. There is excellent camping at regular intervals on this track and all huts are covered by the Department of Conservation's Annual Hut Pass.

Approximate track times:
Makarora to Young Hut (10 bunks): 21.5 kilometres, 7–9 hours.
Young Hut to Siberia Hut (22 bunks): 10.5 kilometres, 6–8 hours.
Side Trip to Lake Crucible from Siberia Hut: 3–4 hours one way.
Siberia Hut to Kerin Forks Hut (10 bunks): 7 kilometres, 2–3 hours.

Side trip to lakes Diana, Lucidus and Castalia: 3–4 hours to Castalia.
Kerin Forks Hut to Top Forks Hut (16 bunks): 13.5 kilometres, 6–8 hours.
Top Forks Hut to Rabbit Pass: 8.5 kilometres, 4–6 hours.
Rabbit Pass to Ruth Flat: 7.5 kilometres, 4–5 hours.
Ruth Flat to Junction Flat: 7.5 kilometres 4–6 hours.
Junction Flat to Matukituki Road: 8 kilometres, 3–4 hours.

Information: Department of Conservation, Private Bag, Makarora. Phone: 03 443 8365. Fax: 03 443 8365.

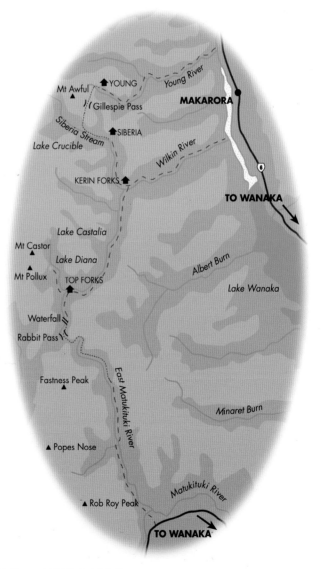

—— Rivers	Over 1550 m		300–1550 m	0–300 m
—— Main roads	···· Routes	🛖 Huts		🪨 Rock bivvy
– – – Walking tracks	▲ Mountains	)(Saddles		

Descending Fiery Col amongst a profusion of snow marguerites (SB).

FIVE PASSES

Gorge and rusting mountains

Modern-day trampers are lucky to have a superb network of huts and tracks in New Zealand, arguably the best in the world, which allow access into country that would be difficult without them. But such facilities are a relatively recent phenomena; it was not until the 1950s and 60s that the present track network was established, initially for deer cullers. Before then only infrequent shelters built by tramping clubs and a few musterers' huts existed, and these were sporadic or absent from the vast majority of the back country. The early explorers had none of these facilities and faced also the uncertainty of an unknown, unmapped landscape – wilderness in its strictest definition.

After completing a few longer trips involving navigation challenges, you might find yourself yearning for a greater wilderness experience – the chance to venture into country where you might gain a sense of what the first explorers felt. Wilderness Areas, of which there are currently seven in New Zealand, provide the opportunity to visit remote landscapes without huts and few, if any, tracks. A classic trip in southern Mount Aspiring National Park, the Five Passes trip skirts the edge of the Olivine Wilderness Area and gives a taste of the harder side of New Zealand tramping. Access is via a tracked route up the Rock Burn – one of the park's most delightful valleys – and then over passes into a landscape of gorges and rusting mountains.

None of the passes are difficult in summer conditions, but competence with map and compass is essential, and there are no huts to rely on for shelter. Modern equipment and a decent map are, of course, major advantages that were unavailable to the early explorers, but there is still a certain romance in choosing your own route and selecting a campsite wherever it suits, and the weather will always be an uncertainty. In wilderness areas you're less likely to meet anyone else, and the experience engendered by the remoteness and solitude can be especially rewarding.

Ironically, the journey on to the little-used Five Passes tramp begins from one of the most popular walking tracks in the country – the Routeburn. A short, ten minute walk on the leaf litter of the benched path leads to a hardly noticeable side track which heads off (un-signposted) into forest on the right. The spacious, tailored expanse of the Routeburn Track makes for a stark comparison to the route you now find yourself on, a weaving passage through beech forest up onto the tops of Sugarloaf Pass.

Sugarloaf Pass gives wide views of the Rock Burn, Mt Earnslaw and the Dart Valley. After stopping to eat and ease cool drinks down parched throats, you begin a descent from the pass which ends above a gorge in the Rock Burn at a signpost marking the route up valley. A few hours alternating between the Rock Burn's forested banks and tussock flats sees you reach the aptly named Theatre Flat. It seems the sort of place from which you could watch the entire drama of the back country – an approaching storm, a

New Zealand's only true alpine bird, the mouse-sized rock wren Xenicus gilviventris *(Nick Groves).*

Tussock flats in the Rock Burn (SB).

falcon swooping on prey, a surging river in flood – if you stayed long enough. The enormous expanse of tussock surrounded by forested mountain flanks and carved by the rippling blue of the river also makes for an ideal camp spot. Camping gives a wonderful flexibility to tramping – there's no pressure to march on to the next hut when a leisurely decision to camp early can be made.

As the tracks in the Rock Burn gradually fade, you're left to your own devices save for a cairn or two amongst the tussock approaches of Park Pass. The views from here are even better than those of Sugarloaf Pass, with the sweeping vista of Hidden Falls Creek running south to Fiordland and the granite peaks of the Darran Mountains. Northward, tarns reflect the slanting faces of Mt Poseidon directly above the pass, and in amongst these are several places to pitch your tent.

At dawn, camped on Park Pass, a heavy dew lay on the nylon of our tent like translucent beads. Hidden Falls Creek was filled with low cloud, which in the dawn light bore an uncanny resemblance to a large glacier, the cloud mimicking the ice which must have carved out the valley over 14,000 years ago. Once the sun had burnt the cloud off, we were able to see the steep drop that would take us into the creek head and the edge of the Olivine Wilderness Area. Venturing deeper into the heart of untracked country provokes mixed feelings; there is the excitement of exploration which verges on exhilaration, but also an uneasy truce with the weather, for should a storm break there is the chance of being trapped by flooded rivers or unseasonable snow. As the chance of a quick retreat becomes remoter, so the awareness of your reliance on your own ability sharpens.

Early morning cloud covering Hidden Falls Creek; the Darran Mountains on the horizon (SB).

Snow marguerites Dolichoglottis scorzoneroides *(Darryn Pegram).*

The steep descent into the head of Hidden Falls Creek requires picking the right bush spur and remaining on it until the valley floor. There is the odd blaze, but as the track is not an official or maintained one, these will eventually disappear. Hidden Falls Creek cascades down from the broad expanse of a saddle dividing it from the Olivine River, and here you first begin to reach the slopes of the 'rusting mountains'.

The Olivines are famous for being centred on a 150 kilome-tre-long band of ultramafic rock which is alternately exposed and submerged in the landscape like the humps of a sea serpent. Most famous are the Red Hills further to the north-west, but Cow Sad-dle and Fiery Col also display broad jumbles of the coarse red rock. Because of the high iron and magnesium content, the vegetation is sparse and stunted wherever ultramafic rock occurs. The head of Hidden Falls Creek divides relatively lush tussock growth on one side, with a desolate, red field of literally rusting boulders on the other. The stark boundary looks like a huge incision in the earth, separating two distinctive Jekyll and Hyde landscapes.

Gradually, the two landscapes merge, losing their sharp boundaries, as Hidden Falls Creek ends at the broad, bovine round-ness of Cow Saddle. Parties often opt to camp here, leaving the ascent of Fiery Col till the following day. It's wise to be cautious when selecting a site, as the saddle is boggy in places and can be-come waterlogged after heavy rain.

As much as one might seek out such remote spots as part of a true wilderness experience, I couldn't help being thankful for some modern comforts. Alphonse Barrington spent some six months pros-pecting for gold in the Olivine area and, without shelter and in constant fear of starvation, conditions for him were without doubt wretched. At one stage, while camped beside a river, he wrote, "This is the most miserable day of my existence. We had to turn out last night at 10 o'clock, and the water rose so fast that we could not get anything away but our blankets... The night was very dark and before we reached the hill I got up to my arms in water. I had to walk up and down all night, the rain still pouring down. If this night does not kill us we shall never die." Modern lightweight tents and dehydrated food mean we can explore with relative ease places which could only be visited in the past through immense hardship and suffering.

Above Cow Saddle rise the flanks of Fiery Col; gashed by a stream lower down, but further up easy enough to cross and sidle along ledges to the final climb onto the col itself. Across the col stretches a red carpet of boulders leading like a tongue into the headwaters of the Olivine River. And to the distant north lies the glistening massif of the legendary Olivine Ice Plateau. Campaigners, who fought for twenty years to have this area gazetted as wilderness (which finally happened in early 1997), wanted most to save the area, centred around the ice plateau, from the intrusion of helicopters and planes, which increasingly diminish the wildness of such remote locations. Even huts and tracks, despite their obvious value in many places, are an anathema to those seeking a true wilderness experience in utterly untouched areas like the Olivines. At the heart of this experience is the philosophy of meeting nature on its own terms.

Although the Five Passes is a relatively easy wilderness trip, the descent from Fiery Col feels very distant from civilisation. In a small group and having encountered no one else, the mountains seem all encompassing, and your party, momentarily, the only people in the world. You cannot experience the sublime beauty of the mountains "without having mind expanded, imagination quickened, soul refreshed, and whole moral being invigorated and strengthened," wrote William McHutcheson, an early visitor to Fiordland.

Having descended the col, the next challenge is to pick a way onto the Olivine Ledge before Fiery Creek disappears into bluffs and a chaos of clefts. The Olivine Ledge runs along the side of the Barrier Range like a window shelf and is dissected by numerous cascading streams, which form swampy patches in many places. Working your way across the ledge's flat tussock wetlands may require a compass bearing in poor visibility, and it's important to pick the correct stream for an ascent to the Fohn Lakes. Being able to read a map as easily as a set of instructions is a prerequisite for wilderness trips. You must be able to understand the steepness of the terrain from contour lines and predict the likely hazards and obstacles.

A distant Poseidon Peak (centre) from above Park Pass (RB).

Remnants of winter on Fohn Lakes; distant storm clouds approaching from the west (RB).

Without huts, home is where you make it; a camp on Park Pass (SB).

The best (but by no means only) route from the ledge follows the true right spur of the stream flowing from the largest of the Fohn Lakes. A spectacular gorge spills through schist bluffs and clinging vegetation, thundering to the lower reaches of the stream. The shelter and extra moisture in such habitats allows a greater diversity of alpine plants to survive, including the Mount Cook buttercup (*Ranunculus lyallii*), large mountain daisies (*Celmisia semicordata*) and various species of hebe. Above the gorge, the ridge narrows and a final clamber over broken blocks of schist brings you to a knob overlooking the outlet of the Fohn Lakes.

Along with views of the Olivine Ice Plateau and the Darran Mountains, the distinctive landscape of the Fohn Lakes is one of the highlights of the trip. During our visit, low cloud raced across the lake in the last light of evening, obscuring not only Sunset Peak but also any sense of scale. The fading light dappled the lake surface and it appeared like a vast ocean cloaked in sea fog. Later the clouds dissipated to reveal a bright moon and the landscape seemed to shrink under the lunar glow. The dynamic combination of changing weather and light on the environment lends freshness to such places each time you return.

Immediately south of the lakes is Fohn Saddle, the fifth and final pass. At 1,506 metres, it's the highest on the trip, and a 500 metre scramble down into the Beans Burn requires care, especially in snow. Running roughly parallel to the Rock Burn, the Beans Burn eventually converges with the Dart River. The tussock flats in the Beans Burn are less defined than those in the neighbouring Rock Burn, with subalpine scrub straying onto the edges like tattered garments. Just past the first band of scrub, a large prominent rock comes into sight on the true right of the river. Here the scrub hides a large boulder field and a careful look amongst the foliage will reveal the best rock bivouac in the area (there are others on the Olivine Ledge and at Theatre Flat). Rock bivvies are natural huts,

Descending Fohn Saddle into the Beans Burn (RB).

the good ones providing dry shelter no matter which direction the rain is coming from.

The Beans Burn bivvy has two different 'rooms', each with separate entrances, and includes a layer of dry tussock for comfort, improvements made over the years by previous parties. During our stay, the rock bivvy became a haven to hole up in during bad weather. While nibbling on crackers we spotted a mouse scurrying amongst the firewood, and two frightened squeaks rang out, one distinctly human. Rodents, for some, make unnerving companions, and usually tend to make use of exactly the same sheltered spots in the mountains as trampers.

Below the rock bivouac, the Beans Burn descends gently enough, and, further down, a track begins on the true right leading through silver beech forest. Silver beech is the most widespread of New Zealand's four *Nothofagus* species and occupies a wide range of habitats from coastal to mountain. Beech trees were amongst the first flowering plants to evolve in the Southern hemisphere and had spread across Gondwana before the breakup of the super-continent some 130 million years ago. Since then, beech has evolved into the different species now found in South America, Australia, New Guinea and New Caledonia. Several beech-associated ferns, lichen and fungi in New Zealand bear striking resemblances to those in Tasmania, Chile and Argentina. One to look out for on your walk down the Beans Burn is the beech strawberry (*Cyttarria gunnii*), a golf ball shaped fungus which parasitises silver beech trees here and also beech trees in Patagonia.

The lower reaches of the Beans Burn become narrower, and a bridge crosses to the true left about an hour above the Dart River confluence. At this point there's the option to spend one more day walking out along the Dart, or the tempting possibility of a jet boat ride – that is if you can reconcile the ironies of ending such a complete wilderness experience on a noisy, mechanised ride back to Glenorchy and civilisation.

Shaun Barnett

Barren talus slopes of ultramafic rock near Cow Saddle (SB).

Silver beech forest, Beans Burn (SB).

FIVE PASSES

Mount Aspiring and Fiordland National Parks

Length: 51 kilometres (with Dart River jet boat), otherwise 64 kilometres.

Time required: 6–7 days.

Nearest town: Glenorchy.

Best time to walk track: December to March.

Fitness: Good fitness required.

Maps (1:50,000): E40 Earnslaw, D40 Milford, E39 Aspiring.

Information: Department of Conservation, PO Box 2, Glenorchy. Phone: 03 442 9937. Fax 03 442 9938.

A wilderness tramp with no huts whatsoever, making a tent essential. Where tracks exist (in the Rock Burn and Beans Burn) they are often poorly marked, and parties must be self-reliant and fully competent with map and compass. There are several river crossings which could be testing after rain, and some parties may wish to hire a mountain radio. None of the passes are very difficult, but as there are five the tramp entails plenty of up and down.

Most of the walk passes through Mount Aspiring National Park, although Park Pass marks the boundary with Fiordland National Park. Between Cow and Fohn Saddles, travel is through the southern edge of the Olivine Wilderness Area.

Snow is likely to linger to early summer on Fiery Col and Fohn Saddle, so carrying an ice axe is advisable. There are good rock bivvies at Theatre Flat, below Park Pass, on Olivine Ledge and in the Beans Burn; exact locations are given in *Moir's Guide North*. With the exception of the boggy and flood-prone Cow Saddle, the camping is excellent.

Access to the Routeburn end begins from the town of Glenorchy where a shuttle bus operates from the motor camp. You can also book a Dart River jetboat from here to pick you up at the Beans Burn/Dart confluence if you don't want the final day's walk out the Dart to the Routeburn.

Approximate track times:

Routeburn to Theatre Flat: 11 kilometres, 5–6 hours.

Theatre Flat to Park Pass: 7 kilometres, 3–4 hours.

Park Pass to Cow Saddle: 7 kilometres, 3–4 hours.

Cow Saddle to Fohn Lakes via Fiery Col: 8 kilometres, 5–6 hours.

Fohn Lakes to Beans Burn via Fohn Saddle: 5 kilometres, 3 hours.

Beans Burn rock bivvy to Dart River: 13 kilometres, 5–6 hours.

Dart River to Routeburn Road via Lake Sylvan: 13 kilometres, 5–6 hours.

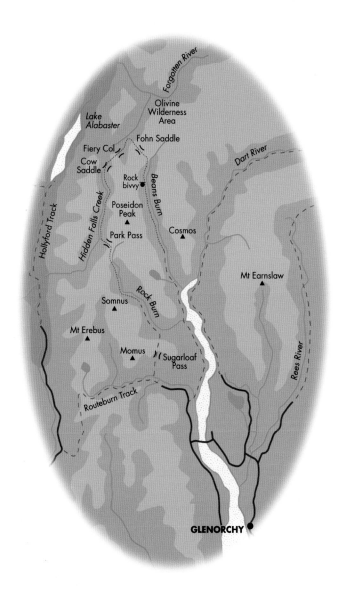

—— Rivers		Over 1550 m		300–1550 m	0–300 m
—— Main roads		···· Routes	▲ Huts		◉ Rock bivvy
– – – Walking tracks	▲ Mountains		)(Saddles		

Aoraki/Mt Cook looms large behind the ridge to Copland Shelter (Nick Groves).

THE COPLAND PASS

Across the land uplifted high

In the summer of 1894–95, there was a frenzy of climbing activity in the Mt Cook region. After many of the major peaks were climbed, attention turned to finding a viable route between Mount Cook village and the tourist attractions of the Fox and Franz Josef glaciers on the West Coast. Following an aborted earlier attempt via the head of the Hooker Glacier, English climber Edward Fitzgerald made the first crossing of Copland Pass with his Swiss guide Mathias Zurbriggen on 25 February 1895. Convinced all that remained was a simple forest stroll to a farmhouse on the West Coast, they consumed most of their provisions shortly after crossing the Main Divide.

Big mistake. Initially they clambered down the giant boulders which choked the upper Copland River in an attempt to avoid the scrub and forest. This was only partially successful and eventually they were forced to confront the tangled gloom of an unknown valley. Fitzgerald described their epic: "It was only with the most violent exertion that it was possible to penetrate at all into this thick maze of underbrush, though it grew no more than four feet high and from a little distance looked quite insignificant. At first we tried to scramble over it, then to crawl under it and, at last, our patience worn out by the stubborn and inert resistance that it offered to us, we began to fight wildly through it, tearing our hands and clothes in the great briars that grew intermingled with the scrub bushes. After almost an hour of this painful and wearying exertion, I discovered we had only progressed some hundred yards." Three

days later, half starved, half in shock, they emerged onto farmland near the coast.

Today, the well cut pack track through the western forest belies the struggle of those early explorers and makes the Copland one of the most accessible valleys on the West Coast. If your ambitions aren't as high as crossing the 2,150 metre pass, then a three day return trip to the head of the valley and back again is still a worthwhile sample of the Copland's rugged beauty.

The Copland Track crosses the most dramatic and rugged part of the central South Island mountains where the land rises from the western beaches to New Zealand's highest summit in a little over 30 kilometres. Prevailing westerly winds slam into this formidable barrier creating two weather affected landscapes with distinctly different clothes.

In the west, life is dominated by an abundance of water. Flowing in from the sea, moisture-laden air is forced up by the mountain barrier, cooling, condensing and jettisoning water droplets onto richly diverse forests. Higher up, the rain freezes and provides regular snowfall to an icy realm of glaciers and névé. The crest of the mountain range forms a natural divide, and once the winds have flowed over this to reach the eastern side they are comparatively dry. Here the montane environment is characterised by an arid beauty where hardy plants eke out a tenuous existence in stark contrast to the rain-drenched lushness of the west.

With suitable alpine experience, the adventurous tramper can

Sunset on the south face of Aoraki/Mt Cook (RB).

125

traverse these two landscapes and enjoy the yin and yang experience which makes the Copland arguably the most spectacular crossing of the Southern Alps. However, the rugged alpine terrain and sometimes ferocious weather can make the journey an intimidating prospect (definitely the hardest tramp in this book).

Most trampers choose to cross the pass from east to west, be-

Scrambling up the loose rock ridge to Copland Shelter (RB).

ginning the journey from the higher Mount Cook village side. The initial graded path skirts around the terminal lake of the Mueller Glacier and follows the Hooker River to its source. A severe flood in January 1994 destroyed much of the track to Hooker Hut, and it is now necessary to head up the side of the Hooker Glacier's terminal lake. With the omnipresent pyramid of Aoraki to the north and the rumbling ice cliffs of Mt Sefton to the south, the struggle up the glacial moraine extends the tramper into a landscape more often the domain of mountaineers.

The climb up the broken ridge to Copland Pass Shelter takes three to four hours and an early (4 am) alpine start will give plenty of time for the long day ahead. Under certain weather conditions you may find yourself emerging from the door of Hooker Hut into a thick, still fog. In this ghostly half-light I find myself imagining the sensation of being submerged within the ice which 18,000 years ago would have completely filled the valley. It's a claustrophobic imagining that I'm not entirely comfortable with, but it makes the emergence through the sea of cloud to the 'other world' all the more liberating. Being high above the cloud brings a great feeling of solitude; but once the cloud burns off revealing the village far below, there's a corresponding decrease in the sense of height and space.

The short, steep section of snow between Copland Pass Shelter and the pass itself is straightforward early in the season but becomes the crux of the trip once the crevasses open up in late summer. It's essential to have the proper alpine equipment for this section: rope, crampons, ice axe, snow stake, sunglasses, prusiks, a couple of slings and, more importantly, the skills to use them.

Providing no clouds have crept up from the West Coast (as they often do on a fine afternoon) and overtaken you on the pass, the hard-won views of the surrounding mountains are incomparable. As you marvel at the vistas, it becomes easier to understand why for millennia people resorted to religion or mythology to explain landforms such as mountains. Even now, with the benefit of scientific knowledge, it is still difficult to grasp the concept of plate

Early morning at Copland Shelter (tracks can be seen leading to the pass on the right) (Elise Bryant).

tectonics which informs our view of such landforms today. Apparently (because to me this is still a mind-boggling fact to absorb), over millions of years the plates that make up the earth's crust have been in a state of constant collision. Combined with the effects of erosion, this intense pressure has forced parts of New Zealand into the raised, folded and fractured landscape that trampers casually refer to as 'the hills'.

From the pass there is still the hill to descend, but height is quickly lost – down snow at first then large plates of shattered rock to the start of a poled track. To the north are the rock spires of Dilemma and Unicorn, and if time permits it's worth pausing frequently to peruse the view and feast on scroggin. In early spring, Mount Cook buttercups sway gently in the afternoon breeze, their enticing dance signalling a return to more hospitable country.

Leaving the zigzags, the track traverses high above the boulders in the Copland River which slowed Fitzgerald and Zurbriggen's descent and passes under the northern ramparts of Mt Sefton. On a fine day, the view rears up a neck-straining two vertical kilometres from valley floor to icy peak. Trying to take in the complete view with a heavy pack on seems like unnecessary effort, and it is simpler to ditch the load and lie down amongst the alpine plants. The aromatic smell is medicinal and like a natural tonic allows the body to forget the struggle up the eastern side.

In benign weather, it is easy to pass through this landscape without any idea of the powerful forces played out through the seasons. I once passed this way in a thunderstorm and the experience gave me an insight that would be hard to gain from reading a book on mountain weather. Within twenty minutes of the heavens

Descending from Copland Pass with the sharp peaks of Dilemma and Unicorn on the skyline (Andris Apse).

opening up, waterfalls had magically appeared from nowhere to lace the surrounding walls. From a distance these appeared, somewhat romantically, as numerous thin silver strands. By the time the flow of water had reached the valley floor, however, the strands had coalesced into three terrifyingly large torrents. The rumble of rocks being pushed down these torrents was ample warning that any attempt to cross would have been foolish.

We took shelter under a large rock, got as comfortable as possible and enjoyed the storm. Luckily, within a couple of hours the rain defied the normal West Coast statistics and eased to a misty drizzle. The waterfalls dried up, the sun eventually broke through, the torrents subsided and, except for the kea which were also celebrating the weather change, some semblance of peace returned to the land.

Waiting for a storm to pass creates an unspoken anxiety experienced by every tramper at some time or other. Fitzgerald described

a similar feeling as their Copland adventure continued: "I could not sleep for the roar of the torrent, as it whirled down past the very rock against which we were lying. It seemed to depress our spirits in a strange way, and kept us awake speculating on the unattractive prospect that lay before us on the morrow."

Further down valley, the scrub which hindered the early explorers is still there, but the benched track makes the experience more akin to walking down an alley. Reaching the pleasant forest glade enclosing Douglas Rock Hut brings a mixture of relief that the hardest day is behind you and sadness that the views will now be restricted by valley walls. But with a fire warming the cosy confines of the hut, a hot brew in one hand and a good book in the other, there is little cause for spirits to be depressed.

A gradual descent from Douglas Rock Hut leads to Welcome Flat and the best hot pools on the coast. Rimmed with orange deposits and lined with a thick sediment of green algae, the pools sit on a silica terrace surrounded by flax and forest. Steaming like three plates of giant green porridge, the water temperature of the three pools varies from too hot to too cold to just right. The green sludge does not detract; the pools are divine! It is standard practice to have started walking early enough from Douglas Rock Hut so that a whole afternoon can be spent turning your skin to the state of a wrinkled prune and adjourning for cups of tea to rehydrate. This cycle should be repeated several times and, if your stamina's up to it, continued well into the day when afternoon mist mingles with the sharp cliffs and spires of the Sierra Range.

The Sierra Range made a big impression on another explorer whose name will always be linked with the Copland. Although very much a freelance explorer, Charlie Douglas spent much of his time in the 1890s exploring both the north and south banks of the Copland Valley with the intention of assessing its suitability for a road linking the popular tourist destination of Mt Cook and the West Coast. In his report to the Chief Surveyor for Westland, Charlie concluded the valley was unsuitable even for mule traffic, but his description of the Sierra Range was more lyrical: "Away on the south side of the flats is one of the wonders of the Copeland [sic], namely the Sierra. The Jagged peaks and broken face of the Wakatipu "Remarkables"; all that I have read or seen of rugged ridges or mountain, sink into insignificance before this wonderful sight. A range of broken shattered cliffs topped by a serrated ridge looking as if some Giant with little skill and a very bad file attempted to make a saw out of the Mountains."

Strangely, Charlie did not mention the hot pools in any of his reports on the Copland Valley. Douglas was very thorough in his work, and during his May expedition steam rising in the chilly air would surely have been a magnet to any inquisitive explorer. My theory is that Charlie Douglas did in fact find the hot pools but the wily old Scot was shrewd enough to use selective reporting to slow the inevitable arrival of tourists. In his dry, laconic writings he often lamented the changes the tourist trade had brought to the West Coast and was wary of those who sought to exploit the land.

Hut is perhaps an erroneous term for the barn-like structure that has been built at Welcome Flat to accommodate trampers. The building has some nice features, but inside large redundant spaces create an atmosphere more often cold, impersonal and un-inviting. These adverse impressions were further reinforced when I read the alarming information panel detailing the rock slide that tore through the lower level of the hut not long after its completion! The hut was then emptied of debris, jacked onto rollers and moved 100 metres east to its present 'safe' location.

Nearby, a large bivvy rock provides an alternative for those hankering for a traditional night's accommodation. Unfortunately, as in most West Coast forests, possums are rampant in the fringes of Welcome Flat and any plans of camping out come with thoughts on how to stop the vermin plundering your gear during the night. The local population is well practised at nightly searches for

Douglas Rock Hut (RB).

trampers' food, and the more persistent offenders seem oblivious to even violent efforts to stop their foul play.

Just when you think the possums have lost patience with attempting to undo your pack straps, the mosquitoes arrive for a midnight feast of your face. Lying awake, trying to remember what possessed us to take the great outdoors option, it was tempting to simply collect up our belongings and waddle back to the hut. But even faced with a tantalisingly close haven, the logical side of my brain went to sleep, leaving the rest wide awake and grimly determined to see out the night in the bivvy.

At first light I stumbled wearily over to the hot pools for an

Alpine herbfield below the northern ramparts of Mt Sefton (Craig Potton).

early morning bath. Some folk who'd spent the night in the hut were already in residence and through my bleary eyes I could jealously tell that they'd all had a good night's sleep. I made a mental note to rethink my opinions of the barn.

The track down the valley to the road end can be done in most weather, although if it has recently rained care needs to be taken crossing Shields Creek half an hour beyond the hut. Initially, the remaining all-weather track stays high and offers only brief glimpses of the river below. Each time I walk this path I am entranced by the way water surges past house-sized boulders and am thankful for the oblique and somewhat removed view from the track. I can sit for long periods of time (or maybe they are short periods, so irrelevant does the concept of time become) simply staring at the action of water against rock as it fights a losing battle with gravity. Even from the relative comfort of the track, it's not hard to see why this landscape attracted explorers with a love of wild country like Charlie Douglas.

From Architect Creek, the Copland's water loses some of its urgency but the flow is still anything but tame. Shortly before the waters merge with the Karangarua River, the track turns inland along an old river terrace and after an hour or so a simple ankle-deep wade across Rough Creek marks the track's end. Standing on State Highway 6 waiting for the bus to Fox Glacier there was once a time when the thoughts of trampers would be quickly turning to mince pies and beers at Fox Glacier (not a great end to the trip for any vegetarians!). Indeed, the wild experience of the Copland Valley has changed little in the 100 years since people first began tramping it – and long may this endure! But I'm also happy that some things do change, and today two excellent cafes at Fox make great coffee and offer cosy surroundings in which to discuss the next adventure.

Rob Brown

130

Welcome Flat hot pools; jagged crest of the Sierra Range in the distance. (Nick Groves).

Copland River (Nick Groves).

THE COPLAND PASS

Aoraki/Mount Cook National Park and Westland National Park

Length: 46 kilometres.
Time required: 3–4 days.
Nearest towns: Mount Cook Village and Fox Glacier.
Best time for walking the track: October to February.
Fitness required: Good fitness required.
Map (1:50,000): H36 Aoraki/Mount Cook.

The Copland Pass is an alpine crossing which requires a relatively high degree of back country knowledge and experience. Since the January 1994 floods, the old track to Hooker Hut has become impassable. The most common way (at present) to Hooker Hut is to follow up the Hooker Glacier beside the terminal lake before climbing the moraine wall to the hut (beware of loose rock in places). This is a fine weather route only. The route from Hooker Hut onto the spur leading to Copland Shelter has become considerably more difficult since the floods. Glacial recession and active erosion means this section is constantly changing; it is recommended parties ask the Department of Conservation about route conditions before they set out. All parties should be equipped with helmets.

It is strongly advised you tramp from east to west. The best time to cross the pass is in early summer (November and December) when the short glacial section to the pass is largely free of crevasses. As summer progresses, crevasses open up and by March can become almost impassable. This area has seen several fatalities which have involved trampers who were not adequately equipped or did not make a cautious assessment of the weather and conditions.

On the western side, there are a number of side creeks which flow into the Copland River which can become uncrossable in bad weather. There are three unbridged creeks between the pass and Douglas Rock Hut as well as Scotts Creek halfway to Welcome Flat and Shields Creek half an hour down valley from Welcome Flat Hut, all of which are flood prone.

A Department of Conservation Annual Hut Pass is valid at all huts except Hooker Hut. Hooker Hut is managed as an alpine hut as part of the Aoraki/Mount Cook system and you will need to purchase a separate hut ticket (around $18) to stay at this facility. There is a comprehensive public

transport system to the Aoraki/Mount Cook side of the track. From the West Coast side, transport can either be arranged, or you can flag down the daily bus service heading along the main highway to either Haast or Fox Glacier.

Approximate track times (east to west):
Mount Cook Village to Hooker Hut (12 bunks): 10 kilometres, 4–5 hours.
Hooker Hut to Copland Shelter (4 bunks): 3 km, 3–4 hours.
Copland Shelter to Copland Pass (2,150 metres): .5 kilometres, 1–2 hours.
Copland Pass to Douglas Rock Hut (2 platforms, equal to 12–14 bunks): 8.5 kilometres, 3–4 hours.
Douglas Rock Hut to Welcome Flat Hut (36 bunks): 7 kilometres, 3–4 hours.
Welcome Flat Hut to State Highway 6: 17 kilometres, 4–6 hours.

Information: Department of Conservation, PO Box 5, Aoraki/Mount Cook National Park. Phone: 03 435 1186. Fax: 03 435 1187.
Department of Conservation, PO Box 9, Fox Glacier. Phone: 03 751 0807. Fax: 03 751 0858.

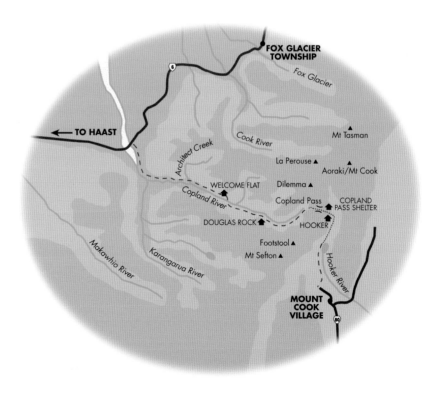

Rivers	Over 1550 m	300–1550 m	0–300 m
Main roads	Routes	Huts	Rock bivvy
Walking tracks	Mountains	Saddles	

WILDERNESS PHOTOGRAPHY

Taking good tramping photographs requires planning, good equipment, persistence, a great deal of hard work and often a little luck.

The part good equipment plays in this equation is certainly important, but can be overestimated. While manufacturers would tell you otherwise, the body of the camera is essentially little more than a mechanism for housing the film and attaching the lens to. An understanding of the basics of photography is always more important than the electronic wizardry presented by the advertisement. Good lens optics are, however, essential. Not only must lenses be sharp, but they must likewise have the ability to faithfully transmit the colour and contrast of varied lighting conditions to the film.

Durable gear is also an essential for wilderness photography – your camera must not fail at the first hint of moisture during a Fiordland deluge! For the record, most of the photographs in this book were taken on Nikon 35 mm equipment, using a range of lenses from 24 to 300 mm. A flash was used sparingly for some wildlife photography; mainly to achieve a natural 'fill-flash' of shadowed areas. A 105 mm micro lens was used to explore the miniature world of plants, mosses and lichens. The heaviest piece of equipment (at over 2 kilograms) was a tripod and this was carried on every trip. In low light, tripods are essential for the slow shutter speeds and small apertures necessary to produce sharp images.

On many tramps, Rob added (to an already bulging pack) a 4x5 view camera, three lenses (a 90 mm wide angle, 150 mm standard and 300 mm short telephoto), fifty sheets of film, five double dark slides and a light-proof changing bag. You need more than a touch of madness to convince yourself (and your tramping companions) that the increased photo quality these can bring will compensate for the extra 10 kilograms of weight.

After equipment, the next most important consideration is film choice. If the intent is to have your photographs published in colour, then positive transparency film (slides) is preferable. Many choices are available, all with their own distinctive qualities and limitations. Fujichrome Velvia was preferred for most of the work in this book because of its exceptional sharpness and colour saturation. But it is a difficult film to use well and has a tendency to look unreal in bright, contrasting light. It is precisely this characteristic, however, that makes it often respond superbly in overcast light. Another limitation of Velvia is its slow speed (50 asa); when conditions required faster films, Fujichrome Provia, Kodak E100S and Kodachrome 200 were used.

Film often records light and colour differently to the eye. In some cases subtle correction was made using 81a and 81b warming filters, which help reduce the blue cast of certain lighting conditions. A polariser was also sometimes used to remove reflections from water surfaces, or to help saturate colours when glare caused problems. Filters should be used primarily as an aid for subtle lighting problems; no amount of filtration is a substitute for that all-too-elusive quality – good light.

Although a certain amount of planning can predict likely combinations of the right location with good light, chance undoubtedly plays a major role. Further, luck favours the persistent. The more you tramp, the more likely you are to chance upon extraordinary light. Good luck!

Shaun Barnett

TRAMPING TERMINOLOGY
A brief glossary

Benched track: a well-formed track cut into a bank or hillside which provides a graded walking surface. Often would have been cut many years ago to provide easy passage for horses e.g. the Arahura Pack Track.

Billy: a light metal container with a long since broken handle which has been replaced with a piece of No. 8 wire from which it is suspended over the fire. Characteristically it is battered, buckled, blackened by woodsmoke and has an ill-fitting lid. Some become family heirlooms which are passed from generation to generation.

Bivvy (and Rock biv): short for bivouac. A very small hut, usually simply constructed, not large enough to stand up in and with just a bare wooden floor to sleep on. A rock bivvy provides a similar style of simple accommodation but is naturally formed by the overhangs of large boulders. The best rock bivs are marked on maps and have been steadily improved over the years by the efforts of visiting tramping parties.

Blaze: an outdated method of track marking which involved cutting a mark on a tree which, however, opened the tree to infection and rot.

Brew: a cup of tea or other hot drink made in the billy.

Bush-bash: off-track in the forest, either intentional or not. In thick scrub, the bush does most of the bashing, trampers occasionally get frustrated and have to bash back.

Bushline: where the forest ends and the tussock tops start. Sometimes a band of thick scrub makes this line a bit vague.

Cairn: an assembled pile of rocks balanced on each other and used to mark routes on tops and in riverbeds.

Cirque: an amphitheatre at the head of the valley, scooped out by the former presence of a glacier.

Crud: 1. bad weather, similar to murk. 2. A nickname given to instant pudding.

Hanging valley: a side valley cut high into the wall of the main valley; usually characterised by a waterfall cascading from the side valley high above down to the main valley floor. Created by the glacial action of a smaller glacier flowing into the main glacier.

Huey: God of Weather. Has a notoriously bad temper, particularly in the Southern Alps and loves to throw rain, hail and snow at trampers, particularly when the weather forecast is for clear skies.

Knob: a high point on the tops which is not significant enough to be called a mountain.

Long drop: a hole dug into the ground some distance from the hut (and waterways) over which a small shelter is built containing a seat with an appropriately sized hole cut out of it. Not so pleasant when the drop isn't particularly long.

Murk: misty, dank weather with poor visibility; especially relevant on the tops.

Permolat markers: a traditional method of marking tracks using 10 centimetre long strips of aluminium venetian blind nailed to trees; usually red, white or a combination of the two. Now being largely replaced by orange plastic triangles which unfortunately do not provide permolat's major safety advantage – the ability to be followed at night.

Pit (and Pit day): the tramper's favourite haunt – the sleeping bag. Pit days are generally cold, wet days where you spend most of the day in your sleeping bag rising only periodically to go to the toilet or make cups of tea.

Plod: an apt description of the slow, steady pace most trampers use to ascend. Degree of elegance used in the ascent is usually inversely proportional to the weight of the pack.

Polypro: short for polypropylene, a synthetic fibre used for warm tops and longjohns. In the last twenty years it has largely replaced wool as the undergarment of choice for trampers but has the unfortunate attribute of smelling bad as soon as you have been wearing it for a couple of minutes. After a week without washing, the garment's smell is fairly offensive.

Route: now used to mainly describe a path of travel which is known and used but not particularly well marked. Differs from a track in that it is easier to get lost and a map and compass become essential. A 'poled route' describes a route on the tops which is often used and is marked with poles to make navigation easier.

Saddle/Pass/Col: all terms for a low point on a ridge which allows access from one valley to the next. Saddles and passes are usually easier than a col. Cols are usually in alpine areas and may require climbing equipment to cross.

Scroggin: a bag of loose snack food which by the second day usually only contains a mixture of nuts, raisins and dried fruit, all the chocolate having already been carefully picked out and eaten separately.

Spur: the ribs which run down off ridges into the valleys. A good way to think of it is rivers divide into streams then creeks; ranges divide into ridges then spurs.

U-shaped valley: a term used to describe valleys in the heavily glaciated landscapes of Fiordland National park and some valleys in Mount Aspiring National Park. The 'U' describes the cross-section of the valley and for the tramper means hard, steep work to get to easier tops.

Tararua biscuit: a highly nutritious homemade biscuit originally designed earlier this century to replace bread as a lunch material on longer trips. There are a number of different recipes but all contain rolled oats, sultanas, golden syrup or malt, and milk powder. Slow baking hardens them for the rough life they are likely to suffer in the pack on an extended trip.

Tarn: a small lakelet or pond usually in the subalpine or alpine zone.

Tops: above the bushline where trampers hope for views.

True right and left: used to describe the left and right banks of any river to avoid confusion in route descriptions. True right is the right hand river bank as you face downstream.

BIBLIOGRAPHY

TRAMPING GUIDE BOOKS

Brabyn, Sven. *Tramping in the Southern Alps – Nelson Lakes to Arthurs Pass*. Brabyn Publishing, Christchurch, 1997.

Bryant, E. & Brabyn, S. *Tramping in the Southern Alps – Arthurs Pass to Mt Cook*. Brabyn Publishing, Christchurch, 1997.

Burton, R. & Atkinson, M. *A Tramper's Guide to New Zealand National Parks*. Reed, Auckland, 1998.

McNeill, Robin (ed). *Moirs Guide South (6th Edition)*. Great Southern Lakes Press, Christchurch, 1995.

New Zealand Mountain Safety Council. *Bushcraft*. Wellington, 1995.

Pickering, M. & Smith, R. *101 Great Tramps*. Reed, Auckland, 1998.

Potton, Craig. *Classic Walks*. Craig Potton Publishing, Nelson, 1997.

Shaw, Derek. *Northwest Nelson Tramping Guide*. Nikau Press, Nelson, 1991.

Spearpoint, Geoff (ed). *Moirs Guide North (6th Edition)*. NZ Alpine Club, Christchurch, 1998.

EXPLORATION/HISTORY

Brailsford, Barry. *Greenstone Trails. The Maori Search for Pounamu*. Reed, Wellington, 1983.

Dawber, Carol. *Bainham - a History*. River Press, Christchurch, 1997.

Jones, J.H. *Fiordland Explored*. Craig Printing, Invercargill, 1997.

Keene, Howard. *Going for Gold*. Department of Conservation, Christchurch, 1996.

MacLean, C. *Tararua - the Story of a Mountain Range*. Whitcombe Press, Wellington, 1995.

Pascoe, John. *Great Days in New Zealand Exploration*. Collins, Auckland, 1976.

Pascoe, John (ed). *Mr Explorer Douglas*. Reed, Wellington, 1957.

Roxburgh, Irene. *Pioneers of Martins Bay*. Whitcombe and Tombs, Christchurch, 1961.

Temple, Philip. *New Zealand Explorers*. Whitcoulls, Christchurch, 1985.

NATURAL HISTORY/GEOLOGY

Bishop, Nic. *Natural History of New Zealand,* Hodder & Stoughton, Auckland, 1992.

Cobb, John. *The People's Park – The Story of Egmont National Park*. Department of Conservation, Wellington, 1987.

Dennis, Andy. *The Story of Arthur's Pass National Park*. Department of Conservation, Wellington, 1986.

The Story of Mt Cook National Park, Department of Conservation, Wellington.

Peat, Neville. *Land Aspiring*. Craig Potton Publishing, Nelson, 1994.

Potton, Craig. *The Story of Nelson Lakes National Park*. Department of Conservation, Wellington, 1984.

Potton, Craig. *From Mountains to Sea – The Story of Westland National Park*. Department of Conservation, Wellington, 1985.

The Story of Fiordland National Park. Department of Conservation, Wellington, 1986.

Thornton, Jocelyn. *Field Guide to New Zealand Geology*. Reed Methuen, Auckland, 1985.

PERSONAL ACCOUNTS OF TRAMPING/MOUNTAINS

Bishop, Nic. *Untouched Horizons*. Hodder & Stoughton, Auckland, 1989.

Houghton, Philip. *Hidden Water*. Hodder & Stoughton, Auckland, 1974.

Pascoe, John. *Land Uplifted High*. Whitcombe and Tombs, Christchurch, 1952.

Pickering, Mark. *The Hills*. Heinemann Reed, Auckland, 1988.

Powell, Paul. *Just where do you think you've been?*, Reed, Wellington, 1970.

Powell, Paul. *Men Aspiring*. Reed, Wellington, 1967.

Radcliffe, Peter. *Land of Mountains*. Methuen Publishers, Wellington, 1977.

Spearpoint, Geoff. *Waking to the Hills*. Reed Methuen, Auckland, 1985.

Temple, Philip (ed). *Lake, Mountain, Tree – An Anthology of Writing on New Zealand Nature and Landscape*. Godwit Publishing, Auckland, 1998.